Living
With
Love

by
KATHLEEN SHERIDAN

THOMAS
MORE
PRESS

Contents

Life with Ed

is

Living with Love

Introduction

I pause with a peculiar tongue-tiedness as I present this book. I say, on the one hand, is it not rambunctious to think I have anything valuable to say about a topic as enigmatic as love? On the other hand, I am convinced of a great need for its discussion. Yes, but am I sure it cannot be said better, more profoundly, perhaps? Will it appear superficial, not worthy of serious merit? Who am I to speak of love?

I am a believer, first of all. I believe each of us has wide and fantastic voyages to pursue in our lives. I believe we are capable of learning many, many things. Loving is the most precious behavior in life. Loving needs to be learned, nurtured, practiced, developed, and experienced. And we have failed, miserably, that charge of teaching. Rather we have commanded imperiously, rigidly, mysteriously that people must love. And we seem inexplicably perplexed when we discover we do not know how.

I believe that love of oneself and deep, moving relationships with others are part of the basic stuff of our human capacity. To not love is not just dismissing a frivolity, a whim, a mere added attraction. To not love is to not live. Life, from my viewpoint, is reaching, seeking, growing, a moving, vital, jarring, animated, explosive adventure. It is never too late.

I am a psychologist, secondly. I work with persons who are experiencing psychological barriers which impede full living of their lives. People in emotional trouble, as well as people who are not, are responsible decision makers. Our task, a client's and mine, is to mutually enter a relationship so that he can eventually come to free, well-predicated choices about living his life. I work with intensely suffering persons; bitter, rejected people; frightened, anxious individuals; those in despair. And we have painfully, ploddingly worked through to growth. People can and do move and change—through relationships like the client-psychologist ones but through many others, too.

Ultimately, I am a lover. An imperfect one. A groping one. But a lover. Each of us is. Each of us deserves to be. Part of my loving is a desire to communicate my belief in it, my belief that love is a highly complex, dramatically deep human experience and mobilizer of our individual quests.

My life experiences are like no one else's. That is true for each of us. Each of us must translate the potential to love for himself alone. We cannot leave its recipe to anyone else. We cannot deny its importance. We cannot pretend we love when we do not. We must not avoid love. People have loved more deeply, more freely than I. That does not negate my effort. Nor must it negate yours.

Living and loving are never far apart.

CHAPTER ONE

Love Is Not . . .

Helene peered through the musty mesh curtains. Dusk was gloving the beach highway and in the background the night-frightened waves were crashing against the shore to escape. Waiting was a scheduled part of Helene's day. Mornings she slept past Mark's awakening, quick shower, and check of his briefcase. He shaved en route. Millie, his secretary, perfected his office breakfast routine, one-half glass chilled, strained pineapple juice, an ersatz croissant with unsalted butter and marmalade. No coffee or tea. They caused circles under the eyes, Mark said.

When the sun burned a bright heat on Helene's body in bed she rose, struggled into her damp bikini and swam a bit. She didn't much like to swim, but somehow felt that telling her friends she swam each morning legitimized her in their eyes. Her body was a stereotype: leggy, unnoticed breasts, long neck, straight hair touching her shoulders, parted on the side. Her skin was brown and tough, creased by hours of compulsive suntanning. Her face was sharp, clear, unmysterious.

She and Mark married after college. His corporation law had been born then, along with two sons. Now, sixteen years later, the boys were off in boarding school, programming themselves for college and professions. The law firm was booming, junior partners, suites of offices, travel, preoccupation.

Helene had raised the boys, had headed the hospital auxiliary, went through golf, bridge, continuing education at the community college. And now on Friday evening as she waited for Mark she was annoyed about Betty's phone conversation that afternoon. "Mark was so appealing when he spoke at the luncheon Wednesday. He made big business so alive and believable. He's into so many exciting things." Helene hadn't known about the luncheon or what Mark was "into."

Around 7:30 the gravel in the driveway crunched Mark's arrival. He entered the house without using any extra steps, still looked impeccably dressed though there were the hated circles under the eyes. Helene offered him his favorite chilled Riesling. Through the steaks and salad, she had wanted to talk but Mark was watching the portable TV. Later she felt warm and wanted as they had intercourse, as they often did on Friday evenings before bed. She wondered if Magnin's would be crowded tomorrow. She wanted to browse and shop awhile, since Mark was leaving for Seattle in the morning. . . .

Romantic? Fascinating? Helene and Mark are drugged; they are robots. Their life is a movie scenario, an article in a magazine, the setting for a TV commercial. They are like paper dolls. The description of them appears somewhat glamorous—wealth, a beach house, his success. But perhaps as we read about them we wish we had what they had, wish we were in their place. It reads so romantically, her yearning for him, her patience. Must not this be what love is all about?

. . . Richard and Diane have been married almost twenty years. They have three teen-agers. Both work. Diane is a telephone operator, going to business school nights to learn shorthand. Richard is a skilled laborer and he also works part-time making local truck deliveries. They have a car and a home almost paid for. They are coming in now to file for divorce, mostly at Diane's instigation. She says she no longer loves Richard, that she has not for a long while, and now that she is becoming more independent she feels it is time to get out.

"What was it like when you loved Richard, Diane?"

"We used to go dancing, go to nightclubs. We laughed a lot. He never drank. Now I don't want

13

him to touch me. I haven't for a long time."

"Richard, how do you feel about Diane?"

"This is all coming out of the blue! What more does she want? I bring home my paycheck every week. I haven't spent a dime on myself for twenty years. I take out the garbage all the time."

"Are you spending less time together than you once did?"

"There's no time together. I bowl once a week, deliver on weekends. Diane's out two or three nights a week. When we're home there're the kids yelling and the in-laws upstairs. And Diane's always coming at me for something."

"How did it used to be, Richard?"

"Diane was a good-looking woman. It was nice taking her to nightclubs, but she lost interest. Same thing with bowling."

Yes, it seems like Diane and Richard have certainly fallen out of love. They have drifted apart over the years, each into a solitary routine, life alongside the other, rarely with each other. Ironically, this tale may be more dangerously familiar than the first one. Have we fallen out of love in our lives? The more critical question may be (surely we suspect so from what we know about Richard and Diane) whether there was love in the first place!

. . . "It happened! It happened!" Barbara nearly collapsed the bunkbed as she plunged into it, knees first, jumping up and down. Her roommate eagerly encouraged her, glad for any reprieve from German literature.

Barbara had been plotting the whole semester to get to Roger. He was so attractive, the way he moved, crew-necked sweaters under open shirts, that thick, rich beard. Luckily he always sat near the front of the room by the windows, so that when Barbara began sitting nearby she neatly apologized with a blush that she was both nearsighted and a daydreamer. Inevitably they agreed to be lab partners. Inevitably (and with a host of clever scheduling) the only time Barbara could work was after the library closed at night. Lingering 2 a.m. walks back to the dorm, too, became inevitable.

Roger was engaged, Barbara knew. She also knew, just from the way they worked together, that Roger was unhappy with his fiancée. You know how you can just sense those things. They never talked about "her." Barbara had planned not to be pushy or intrusive. "Just let him feel I'm really intent on getting a good grade in this course." Christmas vacation crept up. Barbara had decided long ago not to go home, or skiing, or anywhere. She planned to be at the dorm—available just in case. And, of course, she let Roger know that, too.

It wasn't difficult to volunteer driving Roger to the airport. He was spending the break at home with his family and "her." And as he leapt from the car in the jam-packed 5-minute unloading zone, it happened. "I'll really miss you, Barb. Be thinking about you." Exuberantly, Barbara drove her car off the departure ramp and foggily dreamt her way back to the dorm. "He cares. He cares," she repeated as she began to plan for when Roger would return.

Regrettably, Barbara lives in a dream world. Her energy, her whole investment for over four months has been in a fantasy, a creation of her own making. She does not love Roger. She hardly knows him. She is involved in her own manufacture, and she views and interprets the world around her, including Roger's behavior, according to her dream world.

These three vignettes probably jar some memories. We all know several stories about similar couples or Barbaras, only with minor variations on the same theme. We are told these are love stories. What each of our heroes or heroines is going through is an example of being in love or loving. Oh, how much we identify with Helene. She endures and suffers so much. How patient she is!

The story of Richard and Diane may scare us too much, in some ways. But perhaps it doesn't at that. Isn't their life just the way it really goes for everyone? You settle down. You get used to each other. Nothing much changes. You know each other as well as you can. After all, how much more can you learn about another person after being married to him or her for twenty years or so? Even though you don't like some things, you can't change them. Might as well take it easy, wait for retirement, and see how it goes.

Male or female, we can remember as teen-agers the world of daydreams in which Barbara lives. Or perhaps we're still Barbaras—when a glance, a smile, a "how are you," make the day, and at least a week-end's worth of dreams. Without that dream world, life is lonely and empty. There is no more excitement or involvement in our day than the single expectation that soon she or he will notice me and know me.

Love is not so magical, so superficial, so complacent, so happenstance, so destined, nor so painful as the stories suggest. Love, in fact, does not exist in any such familiar tales. What, then, is love?

Love has been the central topic of philosophers, theologians, psychologists, anthropologists since the beginning of recorded time. Love has been nurtured for centuries, guarded, protected, even hidden as one of the great imponderables of all time. Love is all-powerful, we are told. Love is compelling. Love is the reason for life!

The love theme has sold more records, books, films and products than any other known commodity. To be in love is what each of us works for, our ultimate quest. And if we cannot actively be in love in our own lives, we can surely spend the whole of our existence vicariously living the love lives of others. We can weepingly read or see *Love Story* as often as we want. We can watch soap opera heroes and heroines fall in and out of love with a speed that would dazzle the best quick-change artist. We can ponder for ages what Jackie sees in Ari. We are enthralled by Wally Simpson, Brigitte, Ingrid, Warren Beatty, Henry Kissinger. We remember the captivating Valentino and the lone figure who annually places a rose on his grave. Liz and Dick make headlines. The most newsworthy item about the New York Yankees in many years involved the love complications of two pitchers and their wives.

Love, the commodity, supports greeting cards, flower shops, wedding industries, perfume manufacturers, and designers of lingerie. The love theme will sell any product from a toilet bowl cleaner to a heart-shaped-bed honeymoon suite in the Poconos. "He will love you when the house smells fresh as a daisy." And I have always been curious as to how tall people take to a heart-shaped bed.

Love is the noblest of excuses. "I killed her because I love you." "I work late and stay at the office on weekends because of you; I love you and the kids." "I left him because I love you." "I don't care who you are and what you've done, I love you." "I did it, did all of it, just for you." "If I hurt you, it's only because I love you so much."

For something that is so much a preoccupation,

maybe an obsession, there are few subjects so little understood as the subject of love. We are to the point in our society where we *think* we know what love is, as we see it depicted in the movies or on television commercials. We are striving to be like them, dazzling, yearning, and plastic. If we were honestly to believe that love is the way we see it on TV, then unless we are 23-year-old, long-blonde-haired lovelies with gleaming teeth, dating dark haired, over-six-feet, 28-year-old lawyers, we are not in love. No wonder when we see the discrepancy between our own lives and what we see in the movies, we say "might as well take it easy, and see how it goes." There is not much else we could do.

As much and as many complaints as we can attribute to the media and to advertising for making of love a salable item, a profit-making idea, we can also lay blame to more noble, trusted institutions for so many false illusions of love. The early Greeks, our first philosophers, were so ambivalent about love. Greek mythology thrived on tales of love and losses among the gods. Yet, those who enjoyed love were later labeled as hedonists and were accused and deemed to be greatly at fault. Current philosophies hardly even bother to invoke concepts of love to explain the meaning or the utility of life.

Christian religions offer as their bases the two great commandments of love. Religions preach to love God above all else and to love our neighbor as we would ourselves. Their history, however, more often reflects themes and experiences of fear and punishment. As children we unfortunately learned to do things to avoid the wrath of a powerful God, to avoid the punishment of an eternal hell. Often hours were spent by teachers detailing for us the nightmare that was hell, much in the way a horror story is told. If God loved us, it surely was a tentative thing. We learned to be afraid of "him," because more important than a loving God was a God to be feared.

To do things for others, to be kind, was taught to us as being motivated by a spirit of sacrifice—a loss, a giving up, a not-good feeling—not from the spirit or out of the fullness and generosity of love. Somehow we learned that it was painful (or in order for there to be value to it, there had to be pain) to give to others. Somehow we became confused about what it meant and how it felt to love. We began to believe it should hurt and we should feel bad!

Today, some young people are trying to revive the love in religion through various Jesus movements and the joyful atmosphere of "Godspell." But we are skeptical and suspicious of their spirit and enjoyment and disorganization. Perhaps they, and we, will persevere.

Social sciences have attempted to study love,

within their limitations. One obvious drawback to their investigations has been the equation or narrow definition of love to mean mere sexuality. Still we have learned vast amounts about that aspect of love from Freud, Kinsey, and Masters and Johnson. Again, a mixture of fear and sensationalism have caused us to close our ears to the value of what such scientists have explored. The mechanics of sexuality and understanding of sexual drives are important facets to the full adult expression of love. Love, to be sure, is not only sexuality. And certainly sexuality need not include love. But to refuse to understand one facet or the other is a narrowness we do not deserve and cannot condone.

Some social theorists do not believe constructs like love exist at all. There is no proof, they say, that feelings are any more than physiologically-based sensations, or reactions to stimuli in the environment. If love is anything, they argue, it is an increased heart beat, faster respiration, heightened endocrine secretion, all of which combine to yield a positive physical experience in the person. Love is nothing more than that.

Other theorists, humanistic psychologists as they are often called, disagree and say that love cannot merely be quantified by laboratory equipment measuring heartbeat and pulse rate. Love, as an experience, is accompanied by bodily changes (just as all

21

emotions are). But love is more, because human beings are more than just physical organisms. Persons, as self-motivating, thinking, remembering integrators of their own experiences, can shape and change and control their love feelings. But the humanists have failed to make clear and reputable their message. They smack of irresponsible sensualism. Hedonists, maybe? They talk of freeing up oneself to love. But, alas, that mysterious message comes across as a sort of promiscuity. They encourage openness and sharing of relationships. That gets translated into newspaper headlines spotlighting sensitivity sessions and nude marathons.

Love is not, then, a lot of things. It is not a myth. It is not out of reach. It is not out of date. It is understandable. And who can define it for us? We can. No one else. Each individual in his own growthful experience in his lifetime can learn what it is and communicate that learning to others. Living with love is the schoolroom for that lesson. We are each other's teachers and pupils. Living without love is no life at all.

CHAPTER TWO

Learning to Love

Love is unfathomable. It is a great mystery, a force stronger than anything we can imagine. We never quite know when love will strike us. We simply must always be open to it. And when it happens, even though we cannot describe it, we will know it.

There are several fallacies in what you have just read. One of the commonest mistakes we commit is to confuse love or superficially regard it as "romance" or "falling in love." One of the definitions my pocket dictionary gives for "romance" is "any fictitious or wonderful tale." And the phrase "falling in love" connotes a helplessness and lack of any control or say-so in the situation. Love does not particularly fit these meanings. Another fallacy is to consider love as a feeling or an experience that we cannot plan for, cannot understand, cannot learn, have no responsibility for, and cannot make decisions about.

LIVING WITH
LOVE

But very discouragingly, and as we have indicated in Chapter I, what we have learned from philosophy, science and the media confirms for us that to understand love is beyond the individual. It would be too difficult. Perhaps the reason I dwell on this issue so much is that we seem to have been so complacently accepting of this passivity and naiveté in the business of loving.

When children are born, we expect that they will grow up to be "loving" individuals. But how can they do so unless they learn and are taught? Love is not an innate ability. It is not something we are born with and can use when the moment presents itself. We have capacities to love, to read, to be angry at birth but these capacities have to be developed to be useful and actualized within us.

Most parents do teach their children how to love as they are growing up and probably do not realize they are doing so. After all, parents say, "Nobody taught us." Not so. If we love, we have learned how. For some of us the lessons have been very satisfying and rewarding. For others the learning has been most inadequate. Learning to love really does take a lifetime.

Those of us who have attended expectant parent classes or have taken child psychology courses in school may recall the specialness and special needs of the newborn child. Caring for the child does not begin with its birth or even with the pregnancy. Caring should begin well before that, when the couple decides they want to create a child, to invite a new person to share a life with them.

This invitation to life is a most dramatic one. Two people are saying "We want you." That statement is so important because it is so unalterable. It is not like inviting a close friend to dinner or to spend the week or month. It is inviting a person to share a home for years, twenty years, often. And the guest is a fascinating enigma. For quite a while the guest will be totally demanding, totally helpless, and totally ungiving. And we have no idea, as we decide, whether it will be a she or he, tall or short, attractive or homely, healthy or impaired. What happens to that guest, particularly in his earliest growing years, is largely dependent on the couple. What an amazing statement, then, when parents decide "We want you (whoever *you* will be)."

Clearly, the implication is that parents should always mutually decide to conceive a child. One parent, father or mother, ought not to say "It's time to start a family" without involving the other. One partner ought not decide that having a child might save the marriage relationship, or please the grandparents, or provide a companion for an older child, or replace a dead child, or distract from an unpleasant job. Or for any other of the poor reasons that people sometimes have children. *The first step in learning to love is to have been wanted and invited to life.*

Is the reverse, then, an alarming generalization? All children born whose parents did not make a clear choice to have them are doomed? Of course not. But the best of all possible starts to learning and living situations is what we have described.

In all the hoopla and excitement attendant to the birth and life of an infant, the most genuinely awesome aspect is that this is a totally helpless person. His only way of communicating, primitive as it is, is crying. He cries when he experiences the pain of hunger—or the pain of anything. He is totally immobile. He is totally dependent on people, his parents usually, to feed him, to get him around his environment, to keep him from falling, to keep him safe. Rarely, at any other time in our lives, do we have to rely so absolutely on anyone else for our physical existence.

Infants are fairly indiscriminate early on. A mother, a nurse, father, babysitter can feed him and comfort him, just so needs are met and consistently so. In a sense, the newborn expects he will be taken care of—he does not really have any other choice!

As he enters babyhood, the growing person learns to rely on certain people rather than others. Not too startling when we consider that parents are around the most, they care for him the most, and are the most concerned about him. These two people, then, are highly valued and significant, and reassuringly familiar. No wonder then he gets crabby and whiny when he is left with a babysitter. He is frightened and unsure. His familiar, favorite givers are not there. Is she safe? Will they return? *The second step in the learning process is to have felt safe and secure.*

There is some research evidence that if an infant is without a consistent, dependable person (not necessarily a mother or father) for a significant portion of his first year of life, the chances for his growing up frightened and unsafe are greatly increased. If, during his preschool years he loses, by death, illness, separation or divorce, one of his highly valued and significant persons, he will be aware of it (and other people's responses to that loss), react to it, and have to be able to deal with it. We do not want this loss to develop into a reason for him to hesitate valuing another person in his life—lest he lose that person, too.

Parents are amusingly unbelieving as they learn (it's inevitable!) how much their children learn from imitating them. Or how aware children are of how parents are feeling—angry or sad, tense or calm, loving or disappointed. Children learn both from what we say with words and what we say with facial expressions, gestures, and how we say the words.

27

LIVING WITH
LOVE

Children learn this very awareness from parents. After all, what parents would only pay attention to the words as a child answers "no" to the command, "Time for bed," when the baby is fussy and rubbing his eyes and sucking his thumb?

Simple truth. The parent's ability to love will importantly affect the child's learning to love. In other words, parents must not expect children to respond any differently than they themselves respond. Certainly, this learning cannot be a "do as I say but not as I do" phenomenon. "When mother comes into the room and sees me, her face lights up and she rushes over to give me a great squeeze and kiss. She feels good and I feel good. I was just standing here, not doing anything. And still she was joyous to see me." "Sometimes when I am just about to be asleep at night, in my crib, a cool slow breeze lets me know that father has come in. He is brushing the blanket fuzz off my nose and giving me a kiss. There must be something special about me for him to do that. He's warm and he likes me." The baby is learning he is loved.

The child also learns that people do not love all the time. This is a difficult lesson, complex but better learned than not. What if, for instance, his parents never *show* love or *tell* him they love. His conclusion is that they do not love him. No amount of reassuring statements by parents, "Of course I love you, I raised you, supported you, sent you to school," will change that conclusion. Showing affection and telling a child "I love you" are essential steps that cannot be bypassed. If a child sees a mother and father kissing or embracing, or a neighbor child being hugged by his father, and he recognizes he does not get the same responses, he is aware something is amiss. "I must not be lovable, or deserving."

An even more intricate situation exists. A crucial point that we have tried to make is that the child best learns love when he does nothing to *gain* it, nothing other than be his parents' very special guest. He is lovable because he exists, and delights, and reflects his parents. All too often parents teach children they are loved only when they *do* things that parents want them to do. "Mommy will love you if you drink all your milk." "Mommy does not love little boys who cry." "Mommy will love you if you put your toys away."

Teaching children to perform or to eat or to obey because it pleases parents and makes them happy is one thing. Then it is good, solid "positive reinforcement." To teach children that they are *only* lovable when they perform according to parents' expectations is another thing—and very detrimental. The child would quickly learn that if he fails, if he cannot do it, the parent will withdraw his love. "And who am I (what worth am I) if my parents do not even love me?"

When a husband is angry with his wife for a

neglect, a hurt, an omission, a thoughtless act, he feels anger—pain—aloneness. He does *not* feel love. And this is an honest, reasonable state. When a father is annoyed that his son broke his favorite putter, he feels distant and angry at the boy. He does not feel love. Lapses of love between husband and wife, good friends, parents and children are occasional and temporary and certainly expected. Chronic and repeated lapses are danger signals for any relationship.

The point is that we should not demand a double standard from children and expect that they feel what they do not feel. Parents do this a lot, as we know. Take an example. A toddler burns his hand on an open oven door. She is screaming and crying. Mother rushes along and kisses her, reassuring, "Don't cry. It doesn't hurt." How silly! Of course it hurts. It would hurt mother too, if it happened to her. Better to acknowledge, "Of course it hurts. Go ahead and cry. And we'll put some ointment on it to make it feel better."

Another situation. After a heated battle between sister and brother about whose toy it is, brother stomps his foot and says "I hate her. She took my toy." Father automatically replies, "You shouldn't hate your sister. You should be generous with her because she is younger." That certainly is an interesting logic but it in no way reflects the way the boy feels, legitimately feels, when he has lost a struggle or has been aggressed against. How about instead, "I know how you feel, son, and I do admire the way you handled it. Maybe she will be your friend again in a little while." You see, for the moment, just as happens with adults, the boy experienced a lapse of love for this sister with whom he was angry.

These double-standard examples unfortunately occur again and again in some families. The most destructive one I have had to deal with has repeated itself several times in psychotherapy sessions with teenagers and adults. In all cases a parent had died before the child was ten or so. Without exception, each client felt responsible for the death. Each recalled to me a statement made by a grandfather, aunt, mother, or father some time before a loved one died. "You are such a bad boy, you don't love your mother. You hurt her so much you're going to kill her one of these days." What a devastation to the child. What a malicious comment by the adult. What a double standard.

Up until a child is above four or five years old he hopefully is learning to be a "lovee," a recipient of love from his parents. He also observes love relationships between others. Gradually, he begins to imitate expressions of love (which is why it is so essential that there be expressions of love in the family to imitate) by actively hugging and kissing. His first efforts as a "lover" are to give of himself, a small hand in mommy's, a squeeze around daddy's leg, a wet smack on the face of little brother. Note that he does this with people he knows and wants to love. He does not like to love on command (neither do we as adults) and "kiss auntie hello," and chances are he will avoid it under the guise of shyness and embarrassment.

Typically, when children begin preschool or kindergarten they begin to understand the symbolism and meaning of gift-giving. I so vividly remember my first gifts to my parents, to be followed by gifts on Mother's Day, Christmas, Father's Day, and Valentine Day for school years after. I went with my older sister to the 5-and-10-cent store and could barely peer over the counters. Boldly, I chose for my mother a salt and pepper shaker set which cost a nickel. And for my dad, a black comb, diplomatically (even at that age) also a nickel.

I was proud and thrilled and unable to wait for Christmas. I hid the gifts under my parents' bed! Freud would have marveled at that move. Years later when my mom confessed she had peeked, I was alternately understanding and disappointed that she had done so.

One regrettable aspect of gift-giving as a symbol of love is that, again, we have made such a standardized ritual of it. We give gifts at certain appointed times, often without thinking about or renewing the fact that we do or do not love. A gift to a child when he has not done something to deserve it is a special, wonderful treat. Just like a bunch of daisies sent to a husband's office for no other occasion than love is a special, wonderful treat.

From the onset of kindergarten throughout their high-school careers, usually, children will love a great deal, and many people, intensely and really, and with pain of loss and rejection. As parents, not only must we allow it, but we need to encourage it. And in no case may we unthinkingly challenge its genuineness and meaning to the child.

When she is six or seven, her boyfriend will likely be determined by the fact that they ride the bus or walk to school together. When he is 9 or so, his teacher will be the most beautiful, smartest, best-smelling lady in the entire world. When she is 11, she is convinced David Cassidy will pluck her out of a crowd of admirers and claim her as his own. And when they are 14, or thereabouts, life is lived for a glimpse of Sue, a smile by Joe, and lending a book to Jeanne.

As teachers of love, we must never deny the realness of what the child, 7 or 14, is feeling. Of course, some of their attempts are awkward and amusing. Buying baseball trading cards for a fragile 7-year-old girl may not be the most traditional way for our son to express his feelings but it is his way, and it is okay. A 13-year-old daughter's reluctance to run into Frank until her teeth braces are removed is understandable. Not necessary, but understandable.

We know as we look at them that this love will pass, that there will be other friends even though Lois is moving, that Don is probably not the love of a lifetime. We know this but we do not have to tell them that. It is their own experience to learn, on their very own, with our support. That's the way we did it, wasn't it?

When Marilyn has just broken up with her sophomore boyfriend, she wants to eat her meals in her room and listen to the stereo. She may not tell you *in words* that she is very hurt because she has loved very much and been rejected. Let us not say to her "You'll get over it. There are better fellows. You're too young to be in love and be so hurt." What a disrespect for Marilyn's feelings. She has loved as much and been as hurt as she can be for her age, experience, and level of emotional growth. Of course, she will get over it, change, be able to love more when she is 25 years old. But that is completely irrelevant now. Now she needs to have her feelings, limited as they are, understood, respected, and accepted.

Best friends, of the same or opposite sex, are cherished experiences for children growing up. There are pledges of undying loyalty, shared, sworn-to secrets, agonizing absences from each other, and frustratingly long (from our point of view) periods of play and telephone conversations. There are trading of toys and belongings, dinners at each other's homes, exclusive times listening to records (without sisters and brothers barging in), and spats, jealousies, and lapses of love. Some best friends endure from first grade until now; others do not. But no matter. They are such marvelous, intense, valuable events when they occur that what may happen tomorrow is irrelevant.

I remember one of my first best friends, Rosemary. We were quite little, 5 or 6, and we spent days, literally, playing make-believe games on our front porch and in our chair swing. That chair swing was everything, auto, plane, roller coaster, houseboat, one of the three little pigs' houses. We used to break for lunch and eat at her aunt's house.

Her aunt had no children and she would make us hotdog sandwiches. She would slice two wieners, lengthwise, for one sandwich. She would then lay the four halves on a slice of bread, drench them with ketchup (my mother had never done that) and cover with another bread slice. Then she would cut the sandwich in half, again lengthwise, so that the two halves of each wiener remained intact. I was so impressed by that. Somehow that was so special to me;

35

LIVING WITH LOVE

I thought she did it because she had no children and wanted to impress Rosemary and me. Anyway, I was a later sleeper than Rosemary and she would come in the morning. My mom would let her in and she would sit quietly by my bed until I woke. And we would have "milk-coffee" together.

Later we moved and my best friend became Patricia down the street. Patricia turned out to be an even later sleeper than I was. And on summer mornings when I sat quietly and impatiently on her porch waiting for her to wake up I thought what a wonderful friend Rosemary had been to let me sleep. To this day, I regard that, eccentrically perhaps, as an act of friendship—to allow the other to sleep and wait until he wakes up.

CHAPTER THREE

Loving Myself

Of all the intriguing complexities of love, one of its most often misunderstood components is the love of oneself. We are frightened of the very thought. Is that not quite selfish? Most introverted? As the psychologists say, very narcissistic? Is not this just the reverse of what love is really about, putting another person before oneself? Is this not just the opposite of giving, sharing and sacrifice?

In the last chapter we dealt, in various ways, with the fact that parents first teach children that they have a value, a place in life, that they have worth, that they are LOVABLE. We emphasized that such self-value has very little to do with function or productivity. Whether the young boy is a fine ball-player or an excellent student or a poor reader or a finicky eater is relative. A person can possess those characteristics or not; he still is worthy of love. He is unique, special, and precious. He feels good about himself. He has learned to feel good about himself.

He has been taught to feel good about himself.

Sounds ideal. And it certainly is that. In everyone's life and experience, however, the learning is never that straightforward, simple and devoid of problems. One of the more common problems is that lovableness does get confused with my ability to function well. And my ability to function well is typically defined as what will please my parents. For instance, "I begin to doubt myself if my mother is a talented writer and I show no flair and little interest for the literary. Do I disappoint her?" "My father has always wanted for me college and a career. Does he love me less because I enjoy instead mechanics and skills with my hands?" "Compared to my brother's, my marks are not as good. I do not grasp things as easily. I am not handsome. Not as agile. Do my parents love me less? Does my brother regard me highly?" "I am quiet, not very controversial, not too witty, more an observer. Am I less lovable then?" "I understand some things, but I cannot tackle abstract meanings, philosophy and poetry. Is there value to me?"

Other problems crop up that are more beyond my control, even though the result often is that I doubt my lovableness. "My parents constantly bicker and fight. Mother drinks and Father is rarely at home. There is so much anger in this home. Have I caused it? Am I to blame?" "Father and mother are very reserved people. There is little conversation in our home. Voices are never raised; dissension never voiced. Everything is neat and in its place. If we ask questions Father refers us to our teacher or to the encyclopedia. I feel like I am in their way. I bother them." "Mother died when I was born. Dad has not remarried. In fact, he is very sad and misses Mother a great deal. I feel guilty that she died. It should have been me."

And on top of all the possible and probable interferences that will occur in our lives which will cause us to doubt our lovableness, we still wonder what we said in the beginning of the chapter: Is it good to love ourselves?

It is essential. If, as we learn and mature into adulthood, we do not love ourselves, we can never love another in a mature, mutual, sharing, intimate relationship. Only if I appreciate and have respect for myself can I transmit those feelings to another about himself. Only if I acknowledge my own value, do I bring value to a relationship between me and another. If I like being me, another will like being with me. Only if I am secure in my well-being will I be able to go beyond myself and bring something to another.

Loving myself is a marvelous odyssey. It is not, of course, a static event, or something that can be taught in eleven weeks like driving lessons, and never be forgotten. Loving myself is a recurring, continual process of affirming and reaffirming myself throughout my life. It is always being aware of myself and being in touch with myself.

Let us engage in a questionnaire for ourselves. What we eventually decide to answer will be different for each person taking the test. What are the special things about me that make up me? What is my favorite color? If I went into a restaurant and had no money limitations and no weight problems, what would I most like to order? What is my favorite dessert? If I stop now and close my eyes and ask myself, "Am I doing what I like just now?" or, "Where do I really want to be at this instant?" what would I answer?

What do I like about me when I look in the mirror? Color of my hair? My eyes? My shape? My height? My smile? My teeth? Do I like the way I sound? (Of course I have tape recorded my voice.) How do I walk? Am I rhythmic in my gait? Am I a staccato mover? Do I move quickly or slowly? Am I a night person or a morning person? What routine do I go through when I awake in the morning?

What things do I do that delight me, amuse me? Do I ever giggle at myself? Am I ever pleasantly embarrassed, like when I am at an important meeting and discover I and the chairman are wearing the same tie? What do I notice as I walk down the street?

Do I like to talk most of the time? Do I enjoy quiet and aloneness and prefer it occasionally to being with others? When and where do I think best? Am I impulsive or a planner? Am I daring or conservative?

The questionnaire never ends really. Answering it ought to be an exciting compilation of discoveries. The answers ought to generate even more questions and discoveries. But what is the sense of it? Does it matter? Loudly, yes! I am aware of me. I am discovering me. I am observing me. I am understanding me. I am enjoying me!

In answering the questionnaire about ourselves let us hope we are mentally filing away our responses so that we are generating a "repertoire of qualities" about us. Namely, this catalogue of various responses is what is especially me. As I have suggested before, that repertoire should widen, change, and become more inclusive as each of us grows and learns and experiences more about himself and others.

I wonder if some of us might not be uneasy and uncomfortable with this kind of reflection. It is startling to realize how many of us shy away from thinking about ourselves. We do use that silly, misunderstood maxim, "Put others before yourself" as an excuse. As if discovering ourselves, knowing who we are, sensing, perceiving, enjoying, and being aware of it will make us selfish, nasty people like

Scrooge and the Wicked Witch. Ringing in our ears
is that familiar warning that mothers and fathers
used to yell at us when we were teens, "All you ever
do is think of yourself. You never think about anyone else."

Beneath these mildly guilty reluctances sometimes lies genuine fear. Fear of discovering who we
are. We stoutly believe and live as if ignorance is
bliss. "What I don't know won't hurt me." "I
haven't the time for that nonsense." "I have these
proposals to get out." "I'm expected in New Orleans
tomorrow." "The ironing comes first." "The kids
take too much of my time." "With all these exams,
I have no time." "I use my spare time to relax, not
to think." "They are depending on me to finish this
job; I can't stop now." And on and on. Some of us
need all these excuses and many more because we
are so afraid. We are so afraid to face ourselves, to
come to grips with us, and discover if we are satisfied with who we are.

We are afraid of what we do not know, the un-
known, like fearing going to the physician because
we are sure that cancer will be discovered even
though we feel perfectly healthy. We are afraid of
feeling. We would rather avoid it. If we are vaguely
and continually edgy and tense, to stop and consider
ourselves may give us a key to our dissatisfaction
with ourselves. And then we shall have to acknowl-

edge it and deal with it. Again, it is like the way we tolerate a mild toothache or gradually failing eyesight because once we face it we will have to correct it. It is amazing how much pain we endure to prevent what we fear will be even more painful.

All the energy we expend to keep from facing ourselves! Sometimes all the clubs, working overtime, parties, housecleaning, are clever ways of running from ourselves. But the price we pay is dear. Unnecessarily so. We typically are dissatisfied. We rarely really relax. We hardly ever have a genuine, body-shaking laugh. We never lose ourselves into an activity, like being so involved in watching a basketball game that I feel actually scared and responsible when my team is behind by two points and there is less than a minute to go. We probably smoke too much. Chew our fingernails. Shake our foot rapidly and randomly when we "sit still." Cannot sit through a movie. We know how it is to be on the run.

I guarantee that stopping the running and facing the questionnaire can indeed be a relief, first of all. Further, knowing is always better than not knowing. Admitting is better than hedging. And if I have the facts, I am able to take charge and try to do something with what I may not like, or encourage more in myself of what I do like. And, ultimately, I am in charge, whether I admit it to myself or not.

What is me and what is not me? This is not an automatic either-or decision. Remember, many of us have rarely asked the question. And I suspect some readers are answering new questions they have never posed before. Secondly, many of us interpret what is me and what is not me to mean only "what I like about me and what I do not like about me" or "what is acceptable to others about me and what is not acceptable to others." The distinctions may be subtle but they are quite necessary to understand.

Each of us sets standards and goals for himself. Although we are highly influenced by important, and even insignificant, persons in our lives, our standards for the most part must be based on what we want—not on what we think others want of us.

How much energy is consumed and effort wasted trying to be someone else's idea or ideal. "If I do this or that for him, he will love me." "If I go to medical school, girls will be impressed with me." "If I never complain and never make any demands, he will want me by his side." "If I am affable and never argue for my views, I will be accepted by all my friends." "If I volunteer to drive and bring all the beer, this will put me in good stead with the gang. I'll be in." Every example is a potential sell-out of one's own wishes, desires, standards. The aim is to be whatever the other or the crowd might define as acceptable.

LIVING WITH
LOVE

The story about the young starlet trying to make her way in Hollywood is told many times. She doggedly goes from agent to agent, studio to studio, audition to audition. "You are too tall, too beefy, teeth not good, hair wrong color, voice too high, too young, too old." And desperately, the starlet tries to comply. She wants to make herself the product, the conglomerate that "Hollywood" wants. She dyes her hair, has silicone treatments, goes on a starvation diet, pays for plastic surgery on her nose, and takes more voice lessons. She, herself, is hardly recognizable anymore. In our own lives, such transformations are less dramatic and not so total, perhaps, but potentially destructive all the same.

What I like about me and what I do not like about me may or may not correlate with what another person likes about me. That need not be relevant. But here is the point. What I like about me and what I do not like about me *can both* be part of what *is* me and what is accepted by me. For instance, some things about me I cannot change. I am five-feet-five, have brown eyes and wear size 7½ shoes and that is not going to change. I may not like being five-feet-five but it is part of me.

A more difficult example: "I have always admired witty, outgoing people who genuinely attract a group of people. They are entertaining, have a way of holding attention without hogging it or demand-

ing it. They have an easy, likable presence about
them. Alas, I am not that kind of person. I enjoy
humor and am aware of subtleties and ironies but I
cannot initiate their discussion. I am better with only
one person in a dialogue. I get lost with more people
than that and cannot seem to emphasize my points.
I may admire the former style more, but it is not
me."

On the other hand, I am not perfect. Nor am I
willing to be complacent and never strive to improve
myself. There are things I do not like about me that
I am unwilling to accept about me, so I will try to
rid myself of them or change them. "I dislike very
much being overweight. I feel clumsy, lumpy, and
unattractive—and unacceptable to myself. Therefore, with all the anguish and deprivation and strain
involved, I diet and eventually lose weight and get
back to where I want to be."

Again, a more complex example: "I was always
a better-than-average student in high school. I had
majored in business and secretarial skills. I had
always dreamt of having my own apartment and
working until getting married and raising a family.
I worked for several years as an executive secretary.
Quite competent, I often realized that I, in effect,
made many important decisions, anticipated most
problems and kept the organization running very
efficiently. However, I began to see that it was not

challenging to me. I learned the routines and discovered I wanted to be more creative, to test out
ideas in a more flexible situation, to be my own
boss.

"So I decided to do something about it. I began
night classes in marketing. I continued for a few
years and finished my degree with my last year as a
full-time student. I operate a small marketing research and analysis organization now. We generally
work under contracts from larger firms. This is
much more what I wanted to do and I am so glad I
made the move when I did. This is more me."

Still an even more difficult instance: "I knew I was
an attractive woman, nearly twenty-six years old,
enjoying my job. People tended to seek me out. They
responded, I guess, to my good looks, my confident
way of handling myself. But that was typically as far
as it ever got. I never made any friends.

"In college I spent one semester with a roommate,
and from then on requested a single room. I had my
own efficiency studio. I traveled alone, shopped
alone, lived alone. And I did not at all like that about
me. I really felt that something terribly big and potentially very rewarding was missing from my life.
I did not seem to be able to sort it all out. Many men
approached me, but I was aware I acted arrogantly
and angrily toward them. If any of them persevered
through that barrier, it was not long before I became

47

critical of them, argumentative about everything. And so they would stop pursuing. It puzzled me. I felt so deeply that I wanted people, but acted as if I could not bear to be bothered. Could I do anything to change that?

"Clearly, I had to talk with someone about this dilemma. A colleague at work suggested a psychologist and I made an appointment to discuss my questions. I was very nervous and unsure. At least a dozen times I decided I would not keep the appointment and then changed my mind again. I'm glad I went. My therapist and I talked every week for about eight months.

"At times, I was frightened at what I would learn about myself. Some of my fears and doubts caused me a great deal of pain and even more anxiety. But gradually I learned what I was doing and why. And I began to realize that I did not have to act only one way. That there were other alternatives to my behavior. That partly my hostility toward people was an advance set-up so that I could hurt them and protect myself before there was any possibility that I could get hurt. Elaborate, frustrating, but ultimately safe. Eventually I experimented, began to refrain from a few hostile barbs here and there, and I learned. And I began to change what I did not like about me and was basically not me."

I sense a suspicion still lurking, that what we are

discussing here is a bit too Pollyannaish. Perhaps it sounds as if we are searching for idylls among fields of bursting golden daisies, musing on the fascinating, but not-too-relevant issue of loving oneself. A fantasy pastime. How can one really afford such a distraction when meat prices are soaring, when earnings are shaky and jobs are duller, more frustrating, and more difficult to find? There is crisis after crisis in life. Wars precipitate overnight. Can we believe our newspaper reports, our elected officials? Even long-standing institutions. Marriage, for instance, and organized religions are shaky, if not crumbling. These are the issues that challenge, that make us worry, that preoccupy us. This other stuff about the value of self-love is an escapist's pipedream.

Absolutely, the lack of genuineness, trust, and security in our everyday lives is pervasive and abhorrent. We often do not know where to turn. Newscast after newscast is more disillusioning. Women clutch their purses walking down the street for fear they might be snatched. Men and women successful in their jobs tense as they approach middle age, suspicious that younger, aggressive candidates will replace them. Voting in elections appears to offer few choices, perhaps only lessers of several evils.

We cannot distort our concerns and relinquish our priorities, however. We cannot simply demand and clamor that somebody else do something about it.

LIVING WITH
LOVE

We cannot merely complain that, "If only *they* would. . . ." We cannot continue to blame. We need to face the source, ourselves, of our own potential to act, to do, to change things in our life span. Many, many things we will not change. But what we can change begins with our own impetus, our own personal sense of what we want and what we do not want. And unless we know our own assets and liabilities, strengths, likes and dislikes, qualities, desires, wishes, goals and are secure in accepting (loving?) them in ourselves, we will never be able to make legitimate changes in our lives.

I am emphatic in saying that love of myself comes first. If I refuse this, I cannot fully accomplish and achieve. I shall never experience and enjoy. I will be unable to tolerate and tackle challenge and crisis. I will be closed to others and intimacy. I will be static and dull in growth. And there is then no purpose to my life if I am not striving to be aware of myself as the best me I can be. Yes, this love of self, this recognition of the actualizing me, the moving me, the responsive and responsible me, is a powerful, awesome thing.

CHAPTER FOUR

Loving Life

We are a guilty people. I wonder why that is so. I observe that so much of what we want and actually do is filtered and qualified by "I really shouldn't," "I don't deserve it," or "They would be shocked if they saw me now."

Of course, we live according to sets of standards developed and agreed upon through the ages by family and culture, religion and education. When we violate any of these standards, we feel guilty about it and resolve never to stray again. Very silently, however, some of us have accepted heaps of standards thrust upon us without ever having decided whether we *agree* to acknowledge them or not. We have never questioned them nor challenged them. Instead we have allowed them to become imperious and tyrannical. Our lives drift into a series of making sure we do not make waves, we do not step on toes, we do not violate customs. Life becomes a reaction to rules, not an excursion with experiment.

We insidiously begin to anticipate, even before we act, that we are guilty and undeserving, always on the verge of breaking a rule. We are always watchful and careful. Eventually we not only anticipate being guilty, we begin to feel guilty. We are guilty. We do not deserve. How did it ever happen?

Asking a person to define his set of standards is a fascinating experience. Off the cuff, many people will invoke the Ten Commandments. They are safe and all-inclusive, even though the last valid discussion many of us have ever had about the meaning of those commandments occurred in about the third grade. Often, people will respond with the "law of the land." Interesting, but I am not sure what they mean, nor are they. The Constitution? Bill of Rights?

Still others will reflect the standards of their economic class, their neighbors, and educational peers. Thou shalt have a home and two cars. Thou shalt have a bachelor's degree from an eastern university. Thou shalt have a marriage and a boy child and girl children. Thou shalt have white shirts for formal wear. Thou shalt have been to Europe (and not on a tour).

Most of us take onto ourselves our parents' regulations and restrictions. "My house is not truly clean if I do not tackle it as my mother cleaned her home." "My father has always paid cash and my buying on

credit is neither as good nor as noble as his way."
"Children should always spend Christmas with their
parents and if I do not I have not lived up to their
standards."

Probably the easiest trap we set is the impercep-
tive engulfing of our lives into measuring or failing to
measure up to what our parents have said is good and
worthy. We generalize that engulfment to include
rules of the system or the establishment. And, again,
before we realize it, we are reacting in accordance
with a giant rulebook.

Surely, I am not in any way condemning rules of
conduct, disciplines set by parents, and laws of
groups and institutions. What I am concerned about
is the complacency and timidity with which we re-
sign ourselves to standards. We hardly think about
what rules are right for us and which ones are not.
And this is a personal sell-out on each of our parts,
if we have allowed it to happen. The result is that
we have become enslaved, guilty reactors.

Obviously, we should feel guilty about some
issues. Feeling guilty, however, is a result of an act
for which we are responsible, either knowingly or
not. It is the result of an act important enough to
have caused pain or insult to ourselves and others.
It is the result of a violation of our own acknowl-
edged standards. "I am ashamed when I have been
dishonest with someone." "I am guilty when my

wife has wanted something from me and I have not given it." "I am guilty when I have slapped my child out of my own frustrations rather than for anything he did." "I am ashamed when I have not done as well on an exam as I felt I should." "I am guilty when I do not allow myself to enjoy life. *I am guilty when I refuse to take responsibility for my own life.*

"Guilty people do not deserve happiness." "Guilty people do not enjoy." "Guilty people should expect punishment." How many of us live our lives as the sentenced and condemned, afraid to feel happy and enjoy, since we are sure something will occur and it will be taken away from us. The crystal will shatter and we will suffer in the end. That is the way it always happens.

One of the sheer delights of my childhood was the annual school picnic. It was always scheduled for May at a magnificent land of Oz called Forest Park Highlands (long since gone the way of demolition). Early in the year the date of the picnic was solemnly announced and the planning begun. We always had a parade, part of which included class prizes for the gayest banners and most imaginative hats. After the parade, we climbed into buses and shouted "When the Saints Go Marching In" past hoarseness. At the Highlands our families were waiting. My mother, I thought, cleverly arrived early and schemed to get a good table. And she brought potato salad—the only true sign of picnic-time for me. My dad would join us after work.

From the moment I got there I was in a tizzy of activity, the merry-go-round, tilt-a-whirl, ferris wheel, cotton candy, again and again. Near the time my father was to come, I began to sentinel. My plan was to get to him for more money before he heard from my mom how much money I had already spent. It was a thrilling time and I am sure I always needed a few days to recover.

The most prominent memory of the picnics though, and it still saddens me, was this: Every year as I looked forward to the enchanting day, I worried. Surely it would rain on that day and the picnic would be canceled. I would get ill. Or my sister would get ill and then my mom could not go so I would not be able to go. And if any of those disasters did happen, it would be because I truly deserved it. I had no right to enjoy myself. After all, sometimes I had not studied, sometimes I had lied, sometimes I had fought with my sisters, so I should not be expecting to enjoy a picnic. In fact, some of what I felt when I did enjoy the day was that I had gotten away with it and had not gotten caught. Incidentally, though it provided no peace of mind as a youngster, I never missed a picnic.

Some of the residuals of those feelings crop up

now and again for me and I know many of you readers have similar experiences. "We are planning a
romantic anniversary dinner, reservations, wine, just
the two of us. I am sure one of the children will come
down with something." "My first vacation. I've
saved and saved. I have dwelt on travel brochures
and itineraries for a year. I will break a leg, or get
ill, or someone will die and I won't be able to go."

The magic and trickery of such examples is that
we expect punishment and it will be dealt to us
mysteriously and beyond our control. It will be deserved and the end result is that we shall justly
suffer.

Yes, we are a guilty people. Too, we are a bevy of
waiters. We are forever waiting until later. "We
can't go on the trip now but we will later." "Some-
day I will finish high school, not now but later." "I
really should have the checkup but it can wait until
later." "I have always wanted to travel but I'll wait
until I am married, later." "I really would like to
change jobs but maybe I should wait till later." "Our
marriage is at a standstill and I really want to talk
to Jim about it but maybe I should just wait."
"Mom's older and ill and she might die any time so
my plans will have to wait until later." We feel
guilty for what we think we have or have not done
in the *past* and are waiting for something to happen
in the *future*. And we know how to answer the

question, where are we now. We are nowhere.

Religions have unwittingly, and sometimes knowingly, contributed to the waiting phenomena. They reinforce our excuses for inertia. What I am referring to is the concept of afterlife. I am no theologian and have no intention of arguing whether there is or is not an afterlife. We used to call it heaven, or hell, or purgatory, or limbo, although I am not sure the last two are any longer included as possibilities. Whether or not there is an afterlife is not really the point. It is how we have learned to look at the whole issue.

In Chapter I, we recalled how the message of a loving God became waylaid by the omniscient punisher of bad deeds label. Relatedly, afterlife has come to mean solely and merely "eternal reward" or "eternal punishment." It is, in very concrete terms, the final payoff. Life on earth must always be lived in terms of how it is going to be recorded on that final ledger, so we had better play pretty coolly and carefully.

Worse still, we have conjured up an accountant for that ledger and we feel we have gotten advance information on what he thinks are debits and credits. We have decided (through cascades of incredible influences) that our accountant is really heavy on sacrifice and suffering. The more of that kind of thing we do, the better off it will be—later. Life has got to be a series of crosses, borne bravely and silently—because that will look good later. Life is a preparation for later. We must endure whatever befalls us and in the end we shall reap the reward.

I remember a cruel distortion of this ledger business when I was a fairly serious, believing second-grader. Each of us had drawn an outline of a rosary on a piece of white paper, so that each bead could be eventually colored in. We hung the papers on the blackboard in September, our names on them, and they were to last throughout the school year. When we had gotten a good test grade (the teacher decided what was good enough), or when our spelling papers were neat, we got to color in a yellow bead.

When we talked in class, or dropped a pencil, or did not line up straightly for recess, we had to color a black bead. We were told God was indelibly marking those rosaries on His memory. (He could not forget and neither could I.) And years later at the Final Judgment, He would bring that up. I believed that for a time. And I often wondered why we did not get to color yellow beads when I picked up a book someone had dropped, or opened a door for a teacher, or drew a picture for my mom.

I need to make a distinction here, I feel. I am not trying to blame religion. I am trying to stir our own uses of excuses and restrictions and pliancy, our confusing those qualities with goodness and value. I believe in God. Even though I know the definitions of God as First Cause and Supreme Mover, I still tend to use personalized, human adjectives. My God is a lover, an accepting, passionate, active, compassionate lover—who gives and loves freely—and who hears, and understands—and lives and enjoys. And we have made of God a censor, restrictor, a punisher, an excuse.

Where are we now? We are in the presence of our lifespan with the choice to live it or not. We can live it vigorously, actively, passionately, with risks and responsibility. Or we can exist in it guiltily, waitingly, and passively. We can take control of as many aspects of our life as we can, be responsible, enjoy it and love it. Or we can relinquish control to rules, to fear, and to later.

To enjoy life and to love it. This is a difficult concept to discuss. To enjoy means to "get pleasure from." Most of us know that definition. To enjoy also means "to use, to benefit from, to take advantage of." That is the fuller, more active definition, and the one comprehensive enough for our discussion. In other words, to enjoy and love our life is not just superficial experience, suggesting that things went well for us, or we got the job, or he called for a date. It includes experiencing the loss of a loved one, disappointment over a failure, anger in a crisis. "Enjoy" and "love" are active verbs. They mean, here, getting into one's life and moving it.

Learning to love our life entails a series of experiments and experiences, trials and errors. Loving our life can encompass all of what we *do*, our relationship to things, to concrete goals. Yes, loving our life implies that we set goals.

Let us examine our love of life by studying a series of statements about how we operate. *First, I am good at some things. I am able to do some things.* I can work with my hands in carpentry. I can figure a mathematical equation. I can organize a group of people on a project. I can grow vegetables. I can create a sculpture. I can sew a gown. I can shoot a basket. I can iceskate. I can bake cookies. I can write essays. I can balance accounts. I can repair an automobile.

We ought to love what we are able to do, all of the things we can do. In addition, there are probably several things we would like to learn to do. We should enjoy the effort in doing so. We want to compile a repertoire of things we are good at, eliminating things we are not good at, and enjoy the various choices of doing one thing or another. Or at times when we do not always have a choice (like when the car breaks down or the accounts must be balanced at the end of the month), we can still enjoy the fact that we do a thing well.

Secondly, I am a productive person. I enjoy com-

pletion of a task. When I have a job to do, I go at it efficiently. I do not waste time. And I complete the job. I enjoy the *way* I work at the task. And I enjoy the sense of having gotten the job done. For instance, I decided to paint the house, bedroom first, living room last, to use rollers and latex paints. I budgeted a day a room, and I got it done. I liked my decisions. They worked well. And it feels terrific to have finished the painting.

"The foreman gave me two weeks to get this foundation dug before the ground hardens. I estimated the crew I would need and arranged for their time. I checked to have the equipment available at the construction site. Went to the office and reread the blueprints, zoning restrictions, gave the safety instructions. I projected, including possible weather interference, how many days leeway we had if we worked at full capacity pace. We made the deadline, with time to spare. I am very satisfied with the way the job went. We had some things to work out along the way. But it is done and I am glad."

"The term paper is due Friday and today is Monday. Even though it was announced over a week ago, I know that I do not like to work in segments over a long period of time. I like to work closer to the deadline. Let's see. I have three classes today and three Wednesday. I work this evening and Thursday evening. The paper is due at one o'clock on Friday.

Okay, Tuesday morning I'll spend at the library Tuesday afternoon I'll outline and rough draft. Tuesday evening back to the library for more specific research. Thursday, writing and rewriting. And typing Friday morning. That ought to do it. Sounds like a good plan."

The next statement has to do with *goal setting*, short and long-range ones, and accomplishing those goals. Each aspect should provide satisfaction and enjoyment. Goals can have various levels of value and importance in our lives. But setting goals is essential, and reflects a vigorous investment in the way our lives will progress. "I want to go to college." "I want to save for a camping trip next month." "I want to lose ten pounds." "I want to change jobs and pursue a new career." "I want to save for a down payment on a new home." "I want to learn to play bridge." The very experience of entertaining goals can be quite gratifying.

Accomplishing goals that we have set for ourselves is another source of pleasure. This is really what we mean by being successful. Only we can measure our own successes. If someone compliments us on an achievement we did not choose to invest in or was not important to us, the compliment brings a degree of pleasure. But it is not the sort of reaction as when we know we have succeeded at what we wanted and intended to accomplish.

And, of course, we do not relish failure. Failing at what we want is painful and discouraging. It is a result we would like to change and not have happen again. So we assess our goal and its importance again, evaluate our competency and opportunities, analyze our strategies, and decide whether to try again or to stop and do something else. Obviously, the value of goals affects the impact of failure on us. Discovering I will never be able to master the backstroke in swimming is one thing. Failing two or three courses in my first semester of law school is quite another.

I have very deliberately used examples which involved "work," "jobs," "making a living." I did not want any of us to impose artificial dichotomies on the experiences of enjoying life. In other words, loving life does not just refer to leisure time, vacations, and avocational interests. In fact, loving life, to be integral to our feelings about ourselves, refers more to the "work" of our life than to the "play."

There is no question that choices can be very limited in the work opportunities of our lives. Some limitations upon us are beyond our control and some are not. Some of us have not had the money, the desire, or the ability to get higher education, for instance. Some of us began jobs that seemed hopeful but have offered no advancement. Now we are stuck with seniority, retirement payments, and raises in salaries—all of which make changing a job a difficult proposition.

Some of us took the only positions open to us to prevent starving. The choice was as simple as that. Many of us who experienced life during the Depression years understand with great depth that lack of choice and absence of opportunity. Limited as they are, however, and as difficult as they are to attain, some choices do remain open if we vigorously pursue them. Women, for instance, whose children are grown or who never *actively chose* the role of housewife in the first place can make career changes. Older persons who want to change positions or who are at company-determined retirement ages, may invest in job retraining or may involve themselves in community planning and management.

On the other hand, let us not evade the issue of enjoyment for enjoyment's sake. *Experiencing pleasure* is the final statement we should be able to examine and make about ourselves. Again, as with all the loves of our life, its range is vast. One aspect of these experiences is particularly crucial to appreciate, however. Spontaneity, now-ness, full awareness are central. Waiting, past, guilt, later, have but a small place.

The whiff of a flower, the brilliance of sun, the shape of a cloud, the majesty of a skyscraper, the sound of a flowing river, the taste of ice cream, a swallow of beer after a sweaty ball game. The calm of a sleeping person, the smell of breakfast, puddles of rain, shapes and gaits of anonymous people in airports, a mountain, carving a name on a frosty windowpane, the texture of rug on touching bare feet. Flying a kite, screaming for my team to win, challenging my chess opponent, reading a novel at 3:00 a.m., driving in the mountains, fishing for Coho, having a cup of coffee.

Every day contains potential pleasures. Many cost no more than an investment of our own alert and eager awareness. We can learn to love what we love without feeling guilty or needing to apologize. I love television even though it is not "in" to admit so. I relish soap opera and roller derby. I am a Howard Johnson fan; many are not. I like chocolate-covered peanuts, but not raisins. I like live drama, not ballet nor opera. I love watching all sports except golf. I read *Time* magazine, not *U.S. News and World Report.*

"I can go abroad when I am single and not wait until I am married." "The garden needs landscaping but a trip to the Grand Canyon comes before that." "I may have a family some day but I want to buy the two-seater sports car now." "Taking this evening course means babysitters but we can afford it." "Let us not wait until the children are grown before we. . . ."

LIVING WITH
LOVE

Sincerely, I hope each of us is making at each moment, many of these loving statements about our lives.

CHAPTER FIVE

Friendship

It is no secret by now that I am firmly convinced of people's ability to grow and develop and change in order to fully involve themselves in life. In spite of many barriers and limitations, biological and environmental, we are always in charge of ourselves.

We mature at different paces. We can most easily see this diversity in terms of physical development in teen-agers. Heights, weights, voice pitch, sex characteristics, all spurt at different times for different teens. After 20 or so, physical changes continue but typically are not so dramatic. Weight change occurs often after that. But graying hair and wrinkles also appear.

Much more complexity exists in intellectual and emotional development. Curiously, however, we are very insensitive to this fact. We expect, rather magically in fact, that at age 21 (even 18) each person is mature, an adult. At that time we believe each of us is categorically capable of making small or large decisions, in any aspect of life, marital, educational, or financial. And we fiercely demand that we not make any mistakes, at least not visible ones, in the more important matters. No matter how limited or how vast anyone's experience has been, we deem him equally able as anyone else at age 21. Beyond that age we allow little credit or credibility to the possibility that one can change, learn more, or advance in any dramatic way. When we are faced with examples of persons who have done so, we dismiss these incidents as exceptions to our rule.

The real truth is, however, that some individuals at age 18 possess more sense of self, sensitivity for others, and vigor than some people at age 50. Obviously there are plenty of reasons why this is so. The issue really is that it *is* so and we should be accepting of the fact for our own and others' benefit.

Following in this vein, I make what may appear as an intolerant statement. Chapters five and seven have to do with friendship and intimacy. There are, of course, degrees and levels of these experiences. I do feel, however, that certain basic stages of personal maturity must be present before an individual can experience and share in friendship and in intimacy. Let us not interpret this to mean something like "no one under 15 can be a true friend or really intimate because he is not yet mature." That is not the point. Rather, let us realize that some 24-year-olds, some 49-year-olds, some 80-year-olds are not ready to experience full friendship and genuine intimacy. Without question, a person who has not reached the stage where he loves himself and his life cannot experience meaningful sharing with another.

Our discussion in past chapters has in many ways been a prelude, a readying process. Life, our own quest, is a remarkable search in itself. Our life, shared with others, is reaching a zenith, a full, rich peak. There is perhaps no higher quality of human experience than the deepest possible sharing with another person.

We are blithe and cavalier about friendship. "We have been friends for years," says Al, even though he has seen Joe once every 5 years or so. "I want you to meet a good friend of mine," referring to a fellow typist at the office. "You mean Harry Collins?" "Sure, he and I are really close friends." "I didn't even know you knew him." "Listen, this friend of mine, whom I met last night, is going to Aspen with me next weekend."

We call a lot of people friends. Unthinking, we have made the identification "friend" a social cliché. Much as when we say "How are you" to someone, we rarely expect or want a true answer. I wonder what would happen if we sat down and separated those whom we consider our real friends from those whom we "call" friends. I hope we can make these distinctions; they are important ones.

What makes a friend, anyway? *Proximity* at least. Many of our earliest friends lived on the same block. Of course! As children we could not explore any possibilities beyond where we were allowed to roam. How about the kid who sat behind us in third grade? Then there was the girl in my second-period gym class. My lab partner. My first roommate in the dorm. The secretary in the office next to where I work. The guys at the office. The fellows at the plant. Basically, then, the most indiscriminate, or casual, "friendships" are influenced by physical nearness to other persons.

Another factor is *repetition of contact*. A simple factor, actually, is that one needs to see or hear from another person frequently in order to build a friendship. Friendships cease when that contact ceases. There are children and teen-age pals whom I vividly remember. Some I felt very involved with at one time, but once I moved or went to a different school or they did, the involvement ended. We genuinely missed the other, for a time, but later if there happened to be a chance meeting we were aware that we had very little in common, very little to talk about anymore.

A glaring example of what I mean here is the class reunion phenomenon. I carefully avoided my high school reunion. Apparently, I had enough honesty to admit that I had not maintained a sense of camaraderie with my teen-age classmates. Those whose friendships I really valued I was still in touch with. I heard later that it was fun to see receding hairlines and bulging paunches, but that no one had really changed! A highlight of the evening apparently had been the award for the alumnus who had produced the most offspring since high school.

Unfortunately, I was not so self-aware later and cheerfully anticipated my college reunion. Probably I evaded my own insights, because my motives were really to go back and show how much I changed and to parade my husband. The result was a jolt. I should have been more honest with myself. The reunion for me was a roomful of veritable strangers all pausing in an embarrassing limbo, not fully remembering whom and how well we had related to them before and being doubtful as to what this particular event held for anyone in the future.

Perhaps a more familiar experience for some of us is the neighborhood. Proximity and convenience are all wrapped up there. Our demands of one another are minimal and easy. Live within one-quarter of a mile, have coffee perking all day, be able to play poker, gin, bridge, or Jeopardy, be willing to join the car or school transport pool and share a list of good babysitters. Jaded slant, maybe, but again the test often does not dawn on us until after they or we have moved. Typically, there is a card with a note the first Christmas, just a signed card the next, and perhaps none by the third year apart.

Some of us have even had the test of returning to the old neighborhood for a party, after we no longer live there. We review some history between the time we left and now, describe our new home and exclaim about the new sizes of the children. Beyond that is usually a failure to recapture much.

There are probably two issues to appreciate with these examples. First, people who are close by and whom we see frequently can be familiar and comfortable companions. Even so, these factors do not equal close friendships. They could be the beginnings of close relationships but they are not the totality. Secondly, the more honest and aware we are of what people do and have meant to us at various times and places in our life, the less struggle and embarrassment we will be caused later on.

In other words, it is fine, valuable, genuine, and enjoyable to appreciate people at a particular time and place. We need not nor should we expect that appreciation to continue, to grow, or to last beyond that context or contact. Remember what fun we have had meeting and enjoying people on vacations—people we never see again?

It is difficult, if not impossible, at the beginning of

any meeting or acquaintance to predict how deeply the relationship might grow or how long it will last. To use time-limits as reasons for either becoming involved or not involved is to impose unnecessary barriers. On the other hand, to feel the need to put more value on a relationship after it has ended than it actually had while we experienced it is unnecessary and burdening self-deception.

Most casual friendships are time-limited. Especially those based on the types of factors we have already described. For friendships to grow beyond these stages requires special, admitted, *active effort* on our parts. Next we must decide we want to spend time together. We arrange time to be together. This is beyond, say, conveniently riding to work together, or appearing in the same class three times a week, or showing up for the same bowling league.

At this stage we are still tentatively testing out a commitment—of ourselves and our involvement. At this early point in committing, however, we must stress the experimenting and observing that goes on. Here we probably relate to the other by *doing* things together. We are seeing if we are interested in the same things. We bowl, we go to movies, we ski, we play cards, we shop. If at this level we observe enough that we do not enjoy, we end the process. If I like symphony and he prefers hockey and neither of us can stomach the other, we may not explore

anything further. If I am a fiercely competitive card
player and he is a lackadaisical chatterer who cannot remember the bid, chances are we would elim-
inate that activity.

But perhaps we decide to continue. Time spent
gradually shifts from the doing of things to the
sharing of history, attitudes, and goals. "Here is
what I feel about our economic policy and I feel
strongly about it." "I am deeply committed to my
religion and my reasons for it are quite sound." "The
most difficult decision I ever made was quitting that
job; I certainly was taking a huge chance." "I was
never close to my parents and I have always felt a
heavy loss because of it." "If I am not accepted into
graduate school it will be quite a blow. I can't even
bring myself to explore many alternatives now."

What we experience in this phase of friendship is
that we often spend hours talking and talking into
the early morning. We enjoy large parties less and
elect to be with fewer, more mutual persons. We
involve ourselves more often in heated discussions of
differences and work hard at changing the other's
mind or resolving the difference. We probably expend some energy introducing this friend to other
close friends and family and examining all the responses to each other—ever calculating who might
like whom and "what did you think of him?"

Another important shift occurs in the earlier prox-

imity-convenience factors if we have reached this
caliber of friendship with anyone. If I were trans-
ferred or if she moved to another city, with con-
certed effort we could and probably would continue
the friendship. We would write frequently. (I would
not. I would call and regard the value of a friend
higher than the value of an impossible-to-pay phone
bill.) We would, out of desire and effort, visit with
each other, not just on my way to a convention or
business trip.

Our visits would be long enough, not just to review history, but to share our feelings about the
now and future of each of us and to offer enthusiasm, encouragement, or concern about the other
person. We would come away with renewal and
revitalization of the sharing. "It felt good and comfortable to be with you. I planned for it, anticipated
it, thoroughly enjoyed it, missed it since I have re-
turned home, and am glad I called you today to let
you know that."

Let us make a necessary pause here. Our focus has
appropriately been on the process of becoming a
friend and the deepening levels of friendship. We
have dwelt on our movement *toward another*. At the
same time, for there to be a complete relationship
there must be a mutual movement, from the other
toward me. There cannot be a passive or uninterested
partner for a vital relationship to ripen. If that were

the case, the more eager person would withdraw, or agree to let the relationship stay at some less valued, less intense stage.

Friendships are not one-sided. This realization adds to the riskiness of establishing a friendship, to be sure. "I move toward you because I find you enjoyable, lovable, valuable and because I have worthwhile things about me to share." It is up to the other to decide whether he feels similarly. If he does not, I am hurt, lonely, and filled with regret because of the loss. If I am at fault, I feel even more deeply about it and resolve not to repeat whatever insensitivities I performed. If I am not at fault, I do not blame and chide myself for what I could and should have done. Although I am in pain I reacknowledge myself and my value and I eventually continue the movement toward others.

A friendship of the closeness we have described takes time, interest and energy. It yields enjoyment, sharing, learning, peace, and growth. It literally is not possible to have a *lot* of friends at this level throughout a lifetime. It is not often possible to have more than five to eight or so friends like this at the same time in our lifetime. I wonder if you agree with that? Or believe it? I think it is very true. It is such a vigorous investment of self, this friendship is, that to involve oneself in a wide circle of people, I suspect, diminishes the intensity of each relationship or diminishes my own investment in my own self and my work-pleasure.

Pinnacles of friendship, friendships in their fullest appreciation, involve total honesty, commitment, and exclusivity. The history of a friendship, through its first and repeated meetings to its arranged times together, through telling and learning about the other, provides the content, the material, for a deep and important feeling for the other person. That feeling is not automatic, probably is not present, when we first call him a friend. That feeling develops and intensifies the more we gratifyingly and willingly share together. We have grown, mutually, to love each other, through our experience with each other. Love, at first sight, as we know, just isn't.

Now when I am without my friend I miss him. I can probably easily describe his personality to another. I know him well enough to feel his moods, his fears, his excitement without his always verbally telling me. He is, however, free to tell me anything about himself and myself and I am reciprocally free. I can call him when I need his support or advice without prefacing, "I am sorry if I bothered you but. . . ."

On the other hand, he is free to say to me at the times when it is so, and without fear on either of our parts about the hidden meaning of it, "I can't talk to you just now, but I will be there at 2:00 o'clock."

LIVING WITH
LOVE

We can violently disagree, be angry with each other, miss a cue from the other that we should not have been insensitive to, tell all those conflictual feelings to each other and continue the growth of the sharing.

More and more we similarly approach the important things in our lives. Other persons anticipate and expect that we will be together. At the same time, we do not relinquish important individual convictions simply because they are not that highly valued by the other. I do not cease or alter my plans which I have decided are significant for me because my friend is not similarly convinced.

We want to increasingly share more and more experiences together, and learn about them at a similar pace. I never cease to know new things about her or she about me. Silences in our conversation are satisfyingly content, not results of having run out of things to say. I want to be with her, but that does not mean I cannot be without her. It is a choice, not need.

Our friendship enriches us both. It enhances my life. I would do many things to preserve it. I want to always be responsive and sensitive to the other and I expect the same of him. If he did not come through in times of uncertainty or crisis for me, it would deeply disappoint me. I would not expect so much of anyone else. I very much love my friend.

I have deliberately not focused on the inner feelings we have when we are without significant friends, when friends have left us, or when we have left them. Or when we as friends have failed each other. Such times are lonely, painful, insecure times. Eugene Kennedy has written perceptively about these moments in *Living With Loneliness*. One of the reasons I have chosen to avoid discussions of aloneness is because we sometimes tend to use the experience or fear of aloneness to avoid the test and risk of making a friendship. We say to ourselves, "I am afraid to love. What if it ends? What if the other does not love me? Then it will all be over and I will be alone again. What good is it? I have tried before and there is no guarantee it will last. I do not want to be hurt or disappointed again."

You see what happens? We can allow ourselves to fix, not on the relationship, but on being without the relationship so that we are literally not *in* the relationship. We are in the past or the future. And there is no surer way to lessen the intensity of a friendship than to worry about being without it. It keeps us in a constant state of distraction and preoccupation. Friendship is in the here and now.

CHAPTER SIX

Love and Sexuality

Love and sexuality are not synonymous. Yet, some of us have believed they are the same. Or we have never fully learned nor appreciated their differences. It is so genuinely regrettable how little we all know about sexuality just by itself. It can be such a powerful experience. In fact, the very surge of it has in the past frightened away entire cultures, religions, and teachers of morality from its true valid and rich experience. It is a unique and intense human potential, often shackled.

We do not need a treatise on the why's and who's of the paucity or faulty understanding of sexuality in our society. Unfortunately, we can take such facts for granted for most of us. Nor do we need a treatise on the mechanics of sexual behavior and performance. I leave that to the very capable hands of the Masters and Johnsons of our time and the future.

One of the common restrictions reserved for the understanding of sexuality is to define it as only a single experience, namely, genital intercourse between a male and female adult. The problem is that such a definition in no way agrees with our own experiences of sexual feelings. To make it absurdly clear, many of us have never had adult male-female intercourse but we surely have had sexual feelings. Should we not have? Are we depraved? Oversexed? Abnormal? Ridiculous. The definition is inaccurate. Not us. Our fault, perhaps, is again having accepted such a statement without question or challenge.

Let us entertain a broader, albeit less precise, set of meanings for sexuality. Sexuality covers a wide range of feelings and behaviors. Sexuality includes feelings of sensuality and experiences of affection. Sexuality can be felt and not acted upon. Sexual experiences (feeling or behavior) can and do occur without the presence of love in our lives.

Next, let us refresh our memories with some early developmental history. The need for food is essential for physical survival. The human response to that need for nourishment appears to be present at birth. An infant cries in response to his intestinal contractions, a physiological cue for the hunger need. Nourishment, or food, is basic for preservation of life; it secondarily produces a gratifying, pleasurable aftereffect.

As a baby's physical development advances, say, between six months and two years of age, he responds to a different need, to move and master his environment. Thus, he reacts to new sensations in his own musculature. He begins to practice mobility. He learns to walk. He also experiences a sense of gratification over the use of his muscles and over the acquired mastery. We have all witnessed the glee and budding pride of the baby who has just tottered four steps across the room. Later, more refined types of mobility can be mastered with practice. He can jump, run, hop and skip, swim and climb.

If a child could not be mobile, due to some genetic, or congenital, or traumatic physical damage, he could still survive, although in a very restricted fashion. Additionally, we have produced various mechanical substitutes like wheelchairs, crutches, artificial limbs, to aid mobility if such a situation occurs.

Likewise, when a child is perhaps four months or so he begins to respond with pleasure to having his body touched. Stroking or gently rubbing the skin yields a grin. Stroking him behind the ear or on the back of the neck produces sensual pleasure. Rubbing the child in the genital area will also result in pleasure for him. In male babies, stimulation of the penis can produce mild erections. As the child grows, he gains pleasure from even more varied and refined sensual experiences, just like jumping and running are refined mobilities. He likes the feel of wind on his eyelashes, the tingling of hot sun on his arms, a hug, or a massage. He learns he can manipulate his own pleasures in many ways. He can expose himself to the sun. He can rub his arm. He can touch his penis and she can touch her vagina. All these experiences can be gratifying and pleasurable. To be denied the sensual experience that the human being needs and can generate, would create serious physical and psychological restrictions. But like mobility, even with these restrictions, a person could survive.

One of the unique refinements of sexual responsivity that most people first discover occurs anywhere between the ages of seven or eight and twenty or thirty as a result of direct stimulation to the vaginal and penile area. The pleasurable experience is different for each person. However, it can be generally described as a persistent heightening of muscle tension, a gradual intensification of sensual pleasure in the genital area. The peaking intensity of this pleasure includes a rush of sensation through the body, a temporary spasmodic muscle response, and an aftermath of bodily calm or tiredness. This one possible, pleasurable result of sexual experience, then, is called an orgasm. It is not the sole result.

This developmental sketch emphasizes that the potential for sexual experience is no more extraordinary than various other human potentials. It has its unique features, but also develops with similar characteristics of other capacities. As with most of the various activities a person learns he can do, he has control over sexuality, takes responsibility for it, makes mistakes with it, and chooses to utilize it or not. And like most of the various things a person learns he can do, sexual experiences can be a part of a repertoire of lovingness, of himself, or another, or it does not have to be meaningful.

For instance, one of the things I have learned to do is swim. Part of my love for myself may include appreciation of the fact that I have mastered swimming. Part of my love of my life may include the exhilaration and energy of a long, challenging swim. On the other hand, my ability to swim or not swim may have little relationship to my feeling about myself and my life. Swimming may not be part of my loving repertoire.

A second example: Another of the things I have learned is that I can experience sexual feelings. Part of what I love about myself is my own enjoyment of physical affection. I can be free enough and in fact encourage touches and hugs and kisses. Expressions of affection are very meaningful tellings and sharings in my relationships with others. For instance, a man says, "Marie, whom I am very fond of, arouses tender, sensual feelings and I want to share those feelings with her in a physically close way." In other words, sexuality is very much a part of a person as loving friend. On the other hand, this need not be the case at all. He can also say, "The sight of Sophia Loren whom I do not even know, much less love, sparks in me an urgent sexual excitement."

The distinctions between sexuality and love are essential for us to recognize. During teen-age years particularly, when we initially discover that other persons are sources for sexual pleasure, we often mistake feelings of sexuality for feelings of genuine love. A boy's first crush probably has more to do with the fact that Janey has huge brown eyes and long golden hair, and more fully developed breasts than other girls, than whether or not she and he share similar interests.

Perhaps I overestimate too many adults if I limit this mistaking of sexual attraction for love relationship to the teen-age years. I wonder how many of us have been startled to discover that "falling in love" with our dates, our steadies, or our spouses, was not much deeper or more thoughtful than mere sexual stimulation. Love at first sight is an impossibility. Sex at first sight happens all the time. Trevor Howard rushing through war-demolished London to find Irene Dunne, his brief companion in a bomb shelter, may make a popular movie, but it has nothing to do with love. George, on seeing Joanne enter the party with lush thick hair and tongue-touching-upper-lip smiles, may become aroused. But when he says, "I'm going to marry that girl," George has abdicated from common sense. I have often suspected the phrase "opposites attract" was invented solely to try to justify marriage choices made on the basis that members of the opposite sex do physically attract each other.

On the other hand, as matter-of-factly as I can state it, a friendship is not a very important one if it does not include feelings and expressions of sexuality. If I do not experience sensual pleasure from the closeness of our togetherness, I am either avoiding a rich source of enjoyment or I am fooling myself about the meaningfulness of our sharing. If I do not hug, embrace, kiss or caress valued and cherished persons in my life, I am shutting off an essential source of *telling* those persons of my love for them.

Part of our difficulty is this very telling by sexual expression. This telling ought to be as a result of our considered choice and selection. We do not tell just anyone with sexual expression. Again during teen years, the thrill of fondling and kissing often far outweighs the "whom" we are with at the time. That sort of indiscriminateness is expected and temporarily tolerated. But in other ways we actually promote and encourage indiscriminateness and affectionate expression. For example, kisses hello and goodbye are socially demanded customs in some

groups, no matter how well or vaguely one partici-
pant knows another. A drudgery of my existence as
I was growing up was the command that I must kiss
all older relatives, no matter how often or infre-
quently I saw them or if I ever talked to them. Liking
them was not even a matter for consideration.

Severe damage to personal choice and selectivity
comes from clever and cavalier changes of society's
rules depending on the sex of the participants. These
rules have all the whimsical logic of "Mother, may
I?" Girls may, and should, kiss both parents through
their lifetime. Most boys are taught to stop kissing
their fathers at around age ten. Then they resort to a
combination handshake and a ridiculous slap on the
back until the fathers become old enough. Finally,
when fathers are elderly, adult sons may return to
kissing them again. Boys kiss their mothers until
about age twelve. Then after a more or less prolonged teen-age fast, they may again become affectionate. But this affection may change to huge bear
hugs and a bit of tickling while mothers are washing
dishes.

Girls and women can hold hands, kiss each other,
and may embrace when they are excited or when
they have not seen each other for a while. Boys and
men rarely kiss, rarely hold hands. They may be
allowed to embrace, particularly if that embrace is
followed by a peculiar punch at the other's shoulder

and the verbal epithet, "you son-of-a-gun." It may make for humorous reading, but there we have it. We have again yielded to a regulation, one that makes it difficult for us to really tell our feelings when we want to and not tell anything when we are not feeling sexual or affectionate.

We further complicate our freedom to be sexually expressive by some curious "out-of-control" warnings. When we are involved in relationships which are more than perfunctory acquaintances, we invoke cautions that "once you get started, you cannot stop." "Once you allow yourself to be too free with affection you'll end up a prostitute." "It is never 'natural' to be 'familiar' with someone of the same sex." One of the more preposterous, and oddly supportive of Women's Lib, warnings suggests that men cannot control their behavior. Once they begin to be expressive, they cannot stop until they go all the way from a hug, perhaps, to an orgasm, unless . . . ! Unless the woman puts a stop to it. She is his only source of control.

The kind and intensity of sexual expression I experience, and with whom, is under regular control, by myself. We cannot shirk this responsibility, powerful as it may seem to us. We should always choose those to whom we want to show affection. For instance, all relatives do not command affection just because they are relatives. If I like the wife of another couple very much and I do not feel similar regard for her husband, I embrace her and not him when I am with them. All children I know need not be kissed by me. Some of my less close friends I will greet with a warm handclasp, others I will not.

How much and the kind of affection we choose to display to another is a more complex matter. If we really think about it, there are not very many persons with whom we want to be deeply affectionate or deeply sexual. Intense and deep sexuality is a part of very special friendships. We are quite particular and very invested in such friendships. We do not include many people in this category, perhaps only a few in our entire lifetime. This intense sexual sharing in special relationships does not have to include genital intercourse, but often does. So we need not let our concern about "going all the way" hamper our desires for important sexual expression. We, again, are responsible for that choice or not.

What are they like, these feelings and expressions of sexuality? We have alluded to the fact that they range from mild to intensely pleasurable feelings. We have included sensuality, affection, and sexuality in tandem usage. If I conclude I love myself, it would be most contradictory to disregard that I am a sensual being. Remember, I can get pleasure from the sensual me as well as from the swimmer me. Surely if I am five feet two and weigh 200 pounds, those pounds will affect my self-love. I can hardly avoid that weight. If I, most tragically, lose my sight in an auto accident, that loss and subsequent change in my experience with life will affect my love of myself and my enjoyment. We cannot expect, then, that avoiding our sexuality will have no effect on our love of self.

What is the sexual me? First of all, am I pleasing to myself? Am I aware of the beauty of my eyes, the softness of my smile, the curl of my hair, the lilt of my voice, the gusto of my laugh? Are there wintery times when I am dressed in cable knit turtleneck and corduroys and my hair is awry and my cheeks are stinging me, that I feel every tactile sensation? Do I relax in the spray of a shower, aware of the different pressures and temperatures of the water on my toes, my back and my face? Do I like the way I look as I view myself in a mirror undressed? Am I comfortable walking through the privacy of my house without clothes?

When I hear certain musical strains, familiar tunes, or strong staccato beats, do I envision myself as a dancer, or ballet artist? Do I allow myself to move and pirouette and engage my fantasy, however clumsily I perform? Can I get lost in a delicate whiff of cologne or after-shave lotion? Can I still feel the grains of sand and the rhythm of the splashing waves long after I have been to the beach? Do I capture precious memories and revive the glow and thrill that existed then? Do I crave a sauna or a massage at times? Do I enjoy having my fingers caressed?

Do I feel a surge of sensuality as I witness a couple walking hand-in-hand? When I am feeling all right with my world, can I approach my colleague, my roommate, my friend, my spouse with a spontaneous squeeze of delight? Can I kiss someone special to me when there is no particular time, place nor reason? Can I tousle his hair? Can I rest my head in her lap? Can I comfortably hold his hand or walk arm-in-arm?

Do I look at the body of someone special to me? Do I decide what I like and do not like about it? Long legs? Rounded shape? Muscled shoulders? Thick, curly hair? Soft lips? Long lashes? Strong hands? Full breasts? Slim hips? His movement? Smooth skin? Wide smile? Hearty laugh?

What are the most meaningful and enjoyable kinds of affection I can show? A kiss on the eyes while she is asleep? A long, enveloping kiss on the mouth? A warm, full, strong embrace? A gentle squeeze of my arm around his? A back rub? Running my fingers around the outline of her ear? A hug, a lift, and a swirl around? A kiss on the cheek? Noticeable firmness as I shake her hand? We could go on and on. There are endless varieties of affectionate messages.

Any or all of the examples mentioned can produce tremendous pleasurable feelings. We can intend some as light gestures and others as marvelously free and important signs of love. It is not by accident that I tried not to color my samples by delineating the sexes of our expressions, nor the places where many expressions would occur. I wanted not to impose too many restrictions on each person's creativity and uniqueness. We can gather the overall framework, but each of us must then style and experiment with experiencing sensuality according to our own choice and personality.

When we are with someone we love, among the numerous things we want to know about him are the sexual aspects of his life. What are his delights? What does he respond to? What arouses passion in him? What is particularly delicious? What is overwhelmingly exhilarating? What can I learn from his sensuality? What can I enjoy in his sensuality?

A delightful breakthrough in recognizing the variety of ways people can enjoy sexuality together was in the movie *Tom Jones*. The acclaimed sensual scene was a meal between Tom and a wench. We are not attempting to say anything about their relationship. We are applauding the presentation of a mar-

velously uninhibited sexual experience which, in
itself, was nothing more than a meal.

We create sensual situations in our own lives.
Candlelight and soft music is a standard background. Wine and cheese at a picnic is another.
Dancing on a balcony overlooking city lights is a bit
specialized, I suppose. But we need not remain so
glamorous. Shopping together in a supermarket can
be very sensual. Sitting on a subway with my arm
around her is terrific. Bike riding together is another
example. Lying on the sand, side-by-side, is one
many of us recognize. Quietly reading may be another—especially Sunday newspapers. Christmas
morning may be a particular delight.

Simply, no time nor place ought to be excluded as
a potential backdrop for sensual sharing. I do not
personally care to kiss and touch in a prolonged way
in public; that is for us alone. I do smile when I see
a couple hand-holding and hugging, kissing and
brushing hair from the other's forehead. I watch and
I enjoy their enjoyment. In fact, I suspect that those
who are often aghast at "public displays of affection" are fairly envious, unhappy people.

I have never been a poetry sharer, but my husband
and I can eat shrimp and watch Monday night foot-
ball and the sensual aura is the same. A backrub for
me is worth dozens of roses. When I trim my husband's hair, he describes it as a sensual experience.

We feel closer when it rains sometimes. Eating Dairy Queens is our Tom Jones meal. Seeing him in a well-cut suit and tie thrills me. He enjoys me in Levis and bare feet. Even I enjoy me in Levis and bare feet.

Volumes have been written about sexual sharing in marital relationships. The marriage state provides a special opportunity for genital sexuality, the glorious excitement of orgasmic sexuality. Each partner enjoys the right and the thrill of giving and getting dynamic sensual pleasure from the other. There is no such state of doing it just for him because he enjoys it or wants it all the time. Genital sexuality, to have a meaning, is sharing, is mutual and joyous to both. Loving sexuality in marriage is never merely satisfying to one partner and to be endured by the other.

Learning to bring each other to orgasm in marriage takes time and practice. Yes it does! How to enjoy sexual intercourse between two people is not a mysterious happening. Each person is unique in what is sexually stimulating to him. Each couple needs to play, to tease, to practice, to experiment, and to laugh and tolerate mistakes. Fulfillment rarely occurs on honeymoons. Some couples do run into sheer mechanical difficulties with experiencing orgasm. When this occurs, they must discuss it together and perhaps with a third, knowledgeable, person.

Marital sexuality, when it is a part of love rela-

95

tionship, is highly dependent on the status of the couple's intimacy. No matter how often we hear the contrary, a sexual relationship rarely stays intact if other aspects of the relationship are troublesome or stagnating. On the other hand, a thriving rich intimacy in a married couple always includes a playful and rewarding sexuality. Sexuality is part of the whole of the couple. It is not separate.

As we will appreciate in Chapter Seven, the intensity of intimacy in marriages ebbs and flows depending on various factors. Similarly, our sexual experience is not always marvelous and terrific, exotic and alluring. Sometimes our lovemaking is peaceful and calm, very gentle. Sometimes it is a bit matter-of-fact. Other times it is wild, aggressive, and urgent. Still at times it is playful and inventive. It depends on where we are with each other in our total togetherness.

There are many, many ways, and endless kinds of sexuality that we can enjoy in ourselves and others. Probably we have not realized that sexuality can be a part of so many aspects of our life, ordinary or quite glamorous. Additionally there are readers among us who have never understood that sexuality wholesomely and vigorously has a place outside the bedroom of a married couple. If that were all sexuality really meant, our lives would be significantly less rich.

Hopefully, our discussion will confirm what we have always felt about sexuality, that it is integral to our lives. Or maybe it will cause us to rethink our own experiences and perhaps alter them. "I may be quite unthinking with my expressivity. Consequently, no one really takes my affection seriously or specially." "I immediately reject my wife's attempts to engage me in sensual experiences, like how I balk when she prepares martinis before dinner. I wonder why I do that?" "I guess I have always felt a bit guilty about being a girl watcher. Maybe appreciating their beauty and shapeliness isn't so bad after all." "I always felt I had to curb my desire for affection. It never dawned on me that there are many possibilities to expression. I don't have to fear jumping in and out of bed." "Somehow I believed recognition of sexuality in me contradicted my religious and moral beliefs. That certainly does not have to be the case."

Sexuality, then, can be wonderful and good. Sexuality, like enjoyment of myself, enjoyment of the work and play of my life, and enjoyment of others in my life, is essential to my living with love.

CHAPTER SEVEN

Intimacy

Probably the highest, most truly human attainment is the experience of genuine intimacy. There are many vibrant and inspiring peak experiences in our lives. The awesomeness of viewing nature's inventions, the solution of a highly complex intellectual problem, the cure for a terminal illness, the creation of a symphony for all ages, moments of unbridled happiness, and many others. Still, the reaching for the deepest, closest, fullest, committed sharing between people is our ultimate goal. Intimacy is the highest form of love.

There are many levels, many depths in intimacy. It is not an all-or-none phenomenon; either I am intimate or I am not. An intimate relationship typically involves two persons. It is that exclusive. The more each person knows and loves himself, enjoys, gets and gives from his work-play, his friends, the more he loves his life for what it is, the more capable he is of being fully intimate.

LIVING WITH
LOVE

When we suggest that the potential for full intimacy is greatest among adults we are not talking about the privileges of age, like being able to vote at age 18. What we are saying is that necessary preludes to intimacy are many rewarding complex personal life experiences and these all take time to live through—more or less time, depending on the various advantages or restrictions of our family, neighborhood, and other avenues for learning and opportunity. Narrow, limited experiential backgrounds do not naturally lead to full, sharing relationships. Often, when individuals become aware of lacks in their lives, realize that their appreciation of themselves and their goals is tainted by ever-present worry, by fear, and uncertainty (yet how they long to go beyond that state), they often seek out counseling or psychotherapy. These measures can often unravel past and present stoppages of freedom and enjoyment so that the person can continue to look beyond, significantly, to another person.

It stands to reason, then, that all adults do not enjoy nor are they equally capable of intimacy. We may mistakenly equate marriage with the ultimate form of intimacy. It could be, but often it is not. Two lifelong, richly enthusiastic friends could share more intimacy than many married partners I know. Marriage, as we define it, could be a very good vehicle for the pleasure of intimacy, but it is not fool-proof.

It is not fool-proof because we too often go into it
not knowing that one is opting for a state of life
which demands incredible intimacy to make it work.
And many of us who marry are not prepared for
intimacy. We never even thought of it as we planned
to marry another.

The two marriage vignettes in Chapter One con-
tained no intimacy, only cardboard box replicas of being in love and out of it. Whatever the many reasons
we conjure up to enter marriage, one of the few
valid ones is the desire for a full, intimate love with
the other person. I cannot stress too often the fact
that loving, learning to love, is a lifelong striving
for personal development. I have tried to emphasize
this throughout the chapters. Some of us are more
ready, more prepared for intimacy than others. An
important source of support for our statement here
are independent research studies which have found
that the only significant predictor of a good marriage relationship is whether each partner enjoyed a
loving and happy childhood.

It is interesting, I think, to examine again our
societal restrictiveness and lack of understanding
about intimacy. For those of us who have been a
part of the 20's, the 30's, and so on, we have been
characterized as a people who could deal construc-
tively with hardship, with aggressiveness, and with
united purpose. We sacrificed and fought wars,

endured lost lives. At the same time, we were be-
fuddled by and guilty about sexuality, and we experienced enormous difficulties with intimacy.

Those of us who have come later, after 1945, say,
and in the 50's, have rejected somewhat our earlier
values of aggressiveness and assertiveness. We have
espoused the virtues of peace, acceptance, and passivity, forming and stemming from the flower-child
movement. One experience the younger of us have
dealt with much more successfully is freedom of
sexual expression. Ironically, however, the most
important bridge of the so-called generation gap has
been the inability of both the younger and the older
to appreciate and strive for intimacy. It has remained
a perplexity for all of us.

At a widespread cultural level, there truly is an
unbelieving, suspicious attitude toward the positive
enjoyment of the here and now. We discussed this
attitude more thoroughly in Chapter Five. One result
of this prevailing thought, however, is that many of
us are much more comfortable when things go
poorly, when there are crises and problems to be
solved. After all, problems are presumed, expected,
and when they do occur they are no surprise, no
jolt to our routine, no shock to our philosophy that
life is a series of sufferings. Something will go wrong
because that is the way it has always been and that
is the way life is supposed to be. To expect that life

should contain moments of enjoyment, even rapture, is to set oneself up for consistent and sure disappointment.

Therapists, who see clients with problems in understanding and coping with their own feelings, often agree that one of the most difficult emotions for people to express is anger. I think anger is probably the second most difficult experience to cope with. I feel intimacy is the most difficult issue for most of us. Feeling angry (some of us refuse even to acknowledge that we do) is unpleasant enough. We surge and tighten up. We feel threatened and defensive. Discomfort is pervasive. Expressing it is even worse. If I say, "You have really angered me. I resent it. How dare you insult me and ignore my rights in that way," I cannot expect a placid response. What I probably will get is some anger and defensiveness in return. What may occur next may be an intensified, heated argument, lots of shouting. Perhaps the other will cope with our confrontation by denying it, changing the subject, or walking away, or maybe we may work through our differences to reach resolution. One of the typical results of anger, however, is its *distancing* effect. This emotional distance may be temporary until we reach resolution, but at such times we feel untrusting and insecure with the other. Sometimes the emotional distance is permanent. The violation or disagreement is substantial enough so that any relationship, except perhaps the expedient aspects of it, e.g., we have to work in the same office, is ended. Let me say, however, that despite the turmoil and possible consequences of anger, it is essential to our well-being that we have to express it at the time we experience it and to the sources precipitating the anger.

What is the case with intimacy? What makes it an even more difficult experience? Expressing intimacy always involves a risk. None of us is ever completely secure in our lovableness, our acceptability. I think there is no such thing as freely loving and giving intensely to another without expecting or wanting love in return. That is a philosophical whim which has little basis in our real experience. There is always a danger that our expression to another will be rejected. Indeed, most of us have had poignant experiences of loving and being spurned. Only movie characters say, "That is okay, I love you anyway." We real-life people mourn such losses and wonder "if I can ever be lovable to anyone?" Am I willing to risk investing myself in other relationships if it might mean a recurrence of this painful rejection? That experience of rejection is probably the most painful and powerful deterrent to risk-taking and growth that we know of. How many of us have said or heard, "Never again!"

One of the dumbest statements I have ever heard

LIVING WITH
LOVE

is that "Love is never having to say you're sorry."
Another goodie is that "Love is sacrificing yourself
for another." I reject any statements which treat
intimate love simplistically. I also feel such sayings
categorically suggest what a person who is "in love"
should do, how he should act or feel, without including important distinctions. Mutuality is one of
the complex cores of an intimate relationship. Partners in it must be as capable of freely choosing to
enter the relationship as they can be at that point in
their lives. In other words, a person should be rela-
tively knowledgeable of himself, his likes and dislikes, have a message of contentment and enthusiasm
in his life. His seeking of another ought to be as a
result of eager adding and continued growth in his
life. He ought not be primarily seeking another to
avoid facing problems, to escape an untenable living
situation, to satisfy extraordinary needs, to be dependent and cared for, to meet some social standard
of "looking good" in other's eyes, or for other such
detrimental motivations.

Intimacy is a matter of give and take. In repeat-
ing the impracticality of such notions that love is
putting another before oneself and that one does not
expect anything in return, I suspect the opposite is
really more accurate. True love does not continue
unless it is agreed upon, renewed, reaffirmed, and
reinforced. Emotionally, I cannot continue to be in-

tensely involved with a person who does not return that intensity. If I do, I end up in desperation and also in violation of my own love of self. That is, I deserve response. If I persevere in this myth that I need not be loved, I am no longer in the process of loving, I am in the process of punishing—myself. The growthful person says "I want to love. And I want to be loved."

The development of intimacy between two persons follows the same guidelines as the development of friendship. Intimacy is the deepest friendship. Marriage should occur only between two very best friends. If the development of friendship takes time and energy, the continued movement into intimacy takes even more time and greater investment.

The marriage state is a workable setting for intimacy to develop. But it alternately amuses and angers me how little use we make of that potential. Let us take for example the custom of the honeymoon after the marriage has been contracted. Many friends have not had enough time together before marriage to be really able to intimately enjoy all that "enforced honeymoon" time together. Rather they are anxious, self-conscious, and pressured to be at a level of closeness they cannot possibly have reached yet. And if the honeymoon is solely for the purpose of sexual experience with each other, too many of us who are married know the fallacy in that reasoning.

I am deeply troubled, too, when I hear couples complain that "things were so much better back when we were first together." How sad, since they really did not know each other very well then, as well as they do now.

There is so much to discover about the person I love. I want to know everything there is to know, although I realize I can never know him completely. But that is exciting. If I could know all, it would mean he has ceased his growthful reaching in life, he has no new experiences. I wince when I hear long-married couples say that they have run out of things to talk about, that each knows and anticipates everything about the other. How dull and indifferent! My grandfather and grandmother did not begin to travel, and go to dinner and dances until they were about 65. And neither of them could speak English!

I am enraged at advice givers who instruct partners not to tell things to each other, not to be fully honest. "Never let him know that you found the woman's photo in his pocket. Continue as you always have and it is likely that if he is having a fling he will get over it and renew his interest in you." Never let him know! Who else in the world *should* better know than the person you suspect may be losing interest in you? Continue as you have always! Loving him, you mean? Impossible. I am so suspicious, so hurt, so angry, I could collapse. It would not exactly be an everyday happening, I suspect. And if I truly loved him, I could not pretend control and indifference about a situation which is a possible jeopardizing of that love.

Much of the real reason for not being honest has nothing to do with protecting the other's feelings. It is rather to protect ourselves from facing ourselves, from telling things about ourselves that may be so unpleasant as to invite rejection, or from facing conflictual issues between us that would be difficult and painful to confront. Letting issues pass, covered and unresolved, is a sure path to distrust and malignant anger in a relationship.

We fear that being honest with each other will lead to quite unpleasant scenes. We fear honesty less in relating good feelings, although we will deal with some of these reluctances later. Confrontations, angry ones, do and should occur in any intimate relationship. Avoiding anger, never saying anything about it, playing out martyred silences, enduring suspected neglect are all damaging to important relationships. Think about it for a moment. What kinds of situations could make us angry? Ones that are important to us, that we have a stake in. If someone shoves me aside and takes a subway seat I'm heading for, I am annoyed, but it does not exactly ruin my day. If my wife furiously accuses me of making decisions, again and again, without consulting her, I am angry because this is an unresolved issue in our togetherness. Granted it is easier to be annoyed at the seat snatcher. The truth is that people with whom we have an agreed mutual investment have much more chance to anger us. Because we care deeply. With strangers, we can allow matters to pass or be indifferent.

Angry encounters for a couple often result from a misunderstanding, a slight, pressures from other sources that we are taking out on each other. Putting these issues out forthrightly clears the air and focuses the perspectives. Hiding the feelings gives rise to misinterpretations and "blowings up" out of proportion. Some angry confrontations result from significant conflicts in a couple's relationship. One person consistently disregards the other's feelings. A friend continually fails to be supportive of the other during hard times. A wife or a husband is being unfaithful. One person never regards what the other tells him as exclusive and confidential. To not deal with such issues is to admit, really, that the relationship has not much depth and little future. More subtly and more significantly, not to be angry with the other person over conflicts is saying about him that he is not mature and capable enough to deal with them.

How silly it is not to tell each other about other persons who have been important in our lives. We

really don't imagine he has never had any other significant person in his life. I cannot be angry that she
ever enjoyed closeness with another person besides
myself. I realize we are not fully secure, but to avoid
knowing about the important persons of the other's
experience because we would be jealous or threatened is serious insecurity.

My husband first chose to pursue the beginnings
of a relationship with me. In doing so and finding
it promising, he ended a very deep friendship of over
two years with another woman. As he and I became
comfortable with each other, I learned a great deal
about her. Recently I met her. It was a surprising
and reassuring experience. She and I discovered
similarities between us, which of course were obvious but still a discovery. The whole meeting provided a richer appreciation of my husband and, not
incidentally, me. Not wanting to know about her
strikes me as odd as not wanting to know about any
two-year period in his life, like being in school, in
the Army, living in another city, and so on.

I cannot think of anything one partner should
keep from another. The urge to share the silly, the
trivial, the unique, the unsettling, the traumatic, the
routine ought to be active and earnest. This is part
of the reason why intimate friendship demands continual opportunity for contact—the eager desire to
share. There can never be too much time together.

One of my diagnostic clues for marriages in trouble
is how often husbands and wives call each other at
work—never, occasionally, frequently, daily, or
oftener.

It follows, I agree, that duos who do not engage in
a great many conversations with each other are not
close duos at all. Intimacy is not assuming that the
partner knows everything already, or is not interested. Intimacy is loud, not silent. It is motion, not
inertia. It is volatile, not static. It is settledness, not
indifference. It is pain, not avoidance. It is continual
telling to the other.

The development of trust in each other is part of
the growth of intimacy. There are many doubts at
first. "Is she interested enough to see me?" "I
wonder if we will meet again?" "How much does he
care?" Then too, "How will she react if I tell her
this?" "Can I rely on him?" "Will she understand?"
All of us have needed to unfairly test that trust level
with our partners. Again, it is our anxious insecurity
that demands such tests, our partners rarely precipitate them. We push our demands on the other to
unreasonable extremes, almost daring the other to
give up and abandon us. "How wretched can I be
before she will say she wants out?" Thankfully, we
do not often extend such testings for any length of
time.

Trust grows the more I see that my partner acts

as he says he acts, and does so fairly consistently. I am particularly observant of what he says and how he acts toward me. If he tells me he loves me but never spends time with me, what then? If she says I am important to her but keeps putting her work, her trips, her phone calls before me, what does this mean? If he never tells me what I mean to him, where do I stand, what is the contract?

Again, we make these ridiculous assumptions. "He knows where he stands with me. What more does he want?" The only way he knows (and that knowledge is not static: if I am "told" three years ago, this does not mean I should not be told ever again) is if I *tell* him "I love you." "You mean very many beautiful things to me." "I really missed you." "You are beautiful to me." I tell him in things I do. I do not fix eggs just because they are good for him when he really does not like them. I bring him a rose. I offer to drive her to work even though the subway is nearby. I rub her back. I call her every day. I get up first and let him sleep 15 minutes longer. I bring her coffee in bed. I hug him as he shaves. We hold hands as we walk along.

He runs out and starts the car ahead of me on winter mornings. After lavish dinners for friends, he does the dishes. She interrupts her plans because she knows I am upset about something. He comes to a talk I am giving. He cleans bathrooms for me. I

LIVING WITH
LOVE

sew on buttons for him. I buy him a gift because I want to buy him a gift, not because it is a holiday. He says to me, "I love you very much" and I to him, "Me, too, you."

Trust that the other cares for me as deeply as he says he does grows to a point where I know that I can rely on him, that I can freely need him, that he will not leave me, that he will only rarely be insensitive to me, that I shall not have to pay a price of vulnerability to hurt any longer, because I trust him as much as I do.

It is curious how idiosyncratic some of our own personal experiences with learning to trust another can be. I fear sickness, partly because I cannot particularly control it and I enjoy having more control over a situation than I can have over illness. Once I had two embedded teeth extracted. Unluckily and beyond my control, the medication to ease the pain instead attacked my stomach mercilessly. I was frightened, in pain, and extremely uncomfortable and unpleasant since my mouth vomited both blood and stomach contents. I reflected later that through it all, my husband had held my hand or hugged me, never left home even though I was incapable (physically and emotionally) of being a companion to him. Perhaps, for me, that experience represented me at my worst and most vulnerably alone and there he was and he was not going to leave me.

My husband has had a similar significant test. Somehow he had learned that when very important critical life issues occurred, he could rarely rely on anyone for support and that he would have to go it alone. Quite meaningful for him was completing his doctoral dissertation. He was preoccupied with it, nervous, difficult to live with, captive to the approaching deadline, and unusually demanding. Later he told me he fully expected that I would desert him during that period. He was tremendously relieved and surprised that it had not happened at this critical point in his life.

Intimacy is a continual but not a constant growth process. There are peaks and valleys. Peaks occur when I am acutely, quickly, and intensely responsive to the other. When I long for exclusivity and lots of attention to me and you. Peaks are at moments in our togetherness when we are both thinking the same thing and blurt it out together. When we are feeling good, each about his own career, challenges, and progress, and bring the most of ourselves to the relationship. Peaks are when I am my most sensitive to her, when I suspect that she is frightened or troubled about something, and I invite her to share it.

Many issues cause valleys. Job problems. Illness. Concerns for another friend's crisis. Exam times. Outside pressures. Problems with children. A busi-

ness trip. One partner in psychotherapy. Any or all
of these are potential disruptors of intimacy. They
could distance us from each other for a time. These
examples are legitimate obstacles, the natural obstacles that are bound to occur in the life of our intimate relationship.

There are other obstacles, unfortunately, that we
manufacture in order to maintain distance and avoid
intimacy. If we employ these regularly, our relationship is in trouble and we had better face it. Some
couples with children never talk *to* each other, only
through the children. Or there is the "I would love
for us to go but I should really get started on this
report for work." Or "There's so much to be done
on the house I can't afford to take the time off." Or,
"I'm too tired." Or countless, often ingenious excuses for not being together.

Vacations are fascinating tests of intimacy, particularly for married couples. Nonmarried intimate
friends seem to accept more clearly the positive value
of vacations. Excluding the honeymoon routine, how
many of us have vacationed together without the
children? How many only use vacations to visit
friends and relatives? How many of us invite another friend or relative along? How many of us jam-
pack vacations with full-time itineraries so that we
have no free time just to be together?

Many couples are afraid to face the possibility (or

115

want to avoid the fact) that they cannot enjoy each other together. At home we have countless distractions. The work routine, the kids, the ironing, the meeting, the studying, the sleeping—all so that we do not have to face each other. But a vacation—a prolonged time with nothing particular to do! I am rarely surprised when couples in therapy report they discovered how much they argued while on vacation. A vacation together can tell a lot.

Growing in intimacy is always a reaching for more —more depth, more intensity, more sharing, more joy. All of us are capable of more. I hope many of us can say, though, that "now, at this time in my life, I am involved as intimately as I am able to be." Intimacy is not a balanced affair. No matter how agreed the mutuality, each of us is an individual who has strengths and still some weaknesses. Both partners do not and cannot always invest to the same degree and in the same way. Each of us has short-comings which, hopefully, we are both aware of. Hopefully, too, we are working at them.

My husband is freer, less protected than I. I am more creative, more curious than he. He is gentler, more open. At times, I have been so concerned about my fears, my safety, that I have disregarded him. At times, we have both put our careers before the other. He is more patient than I. I am more efficient than he. We compete with each other. At times he does not hear me. He is more approachable and perceptive than I. He is more active. I am more reflective. We are not always where we want each other to be.

Joy, excitement, contentment, eagerness, a bit of fear, all preside when intimacy is alive. Drudgery tasks, dull jobs, other problems do not dissolve or magically change when persons are intimate. They are still present, but they exist in a context where something more rewarding, more meaningful, more valuable exists in my life. Consequently, I can deal with these issues and they will not overwhelm me. I can tolerate them if I must, and I will not allow them to gain importance out of proportion.

Intimacy results, necessarily so, in a series of priorities regarding other people in our lives. If I am truly intimate with one person or with two or three, these experiences reward my good feelings about myself. Thus, I am free to engage many more people. Intimacy generates even more going toward others, not at equal levels of importance and meaning, however. But it does orient us more positively toward others.

By its very nature, however, intimacy with one person precludes many other concurrent intimate relationships. How can I possibly invest all that I do with several people at one time? I simply cannot. Therefore, I am suspicious when someone proclaims that he is intimately involved with many people. I am more than suspicious. I downright do not believe him. He does not know what intimacy is.

I and my intimate partner tend, as we grow, to invite others into our sharing whom we mutually like and enjoy. Occasionally, one of us befriends a person who generally disinterests our partner. When this would happen we would not impose the second friendship on the other person, insist that he invest in it, too. We would pursue that relationship freely and on our own. There would rarely occur a relationship which one partner enjoys that would violate or threaten our most cherished, our most highly-prized togetherness. Such would necessarily follow, if the elements of intimacy are truly operative in our lives.

I have a sense of "unfinishedness" about our discussion, probably because there can be no end to this story. There are countless other aspects to experiences and expressions of love, that philosophy and psychology cannot tell you, that I cannot tell you, that television cannot tell you. These countless facts are for each of us to discover and cherish in our own reaching out. Precious moments—gasps of breath, waiting smiles, chills of excitement, sighs of completeness, relief from a fear—are open for each of us to experience, ourselves and with another.